AF007364

40 YEARS OF BLOODROOT
essays by Selma Miriam & Noel Furie
photographs by Noel Furie
edited & designed by Emily Larned

Our daily lives have to be a satisfaction in themselves

2020

Feminism— what is feminism
...ings to different women. Some of
...e legitimacy... wom...
...

...waiter resta...
...their places as
...ants as they
...with culinary institute tra...
...wait sta... ...ree the s...
...s that s... ...d place
...? The... ...esta...
...n the sev... ...d, mac
...Buddh... ...e and
...egetarian ...inist>
...out wa... ...they a...
...wait ...and w
...bused.
...them to

> Our daily lives have to be Satisfaction in themselves

TABLE OF CONTENTS

Editor's Introduction   6
Bloodroot Chronology   8
Building Bloodroot   10

Bloodroot: Brewing Visions   18

The Political Palate
Introduction   42
Some Notes on the Passage of the Seasons . . .   52

The Second Seasonal Political Palate
Feminism in the Eighties   56
Ethical Vegetarianism   62
On Collectivity & Work   70
A Witch Recipe for Grievers   78

Part-Time Bloodroot   82

The Perennial Political Palate
On Persistence & Feminism   90

Personal Essays
Her Life & Mine   120
A Consideration of the Domestic Arts   132

On these opening pages, portraits by Noel from the early days of Bloodroot:

Clockwise from left: Part-time workers Alicia Woodson, Charlene LaVoie, Dawn McDaniel.

Inside front cover, clockwise from left: feminist figures Batya Bauman & Phyllis Chesler; self-portrait; photographer Beth Karbe; part-time worker Jill Harker; jazz guitarist Mimi Fox; herbalist Billie Potts.

It is not easy to demand the most from ourselves—from our lives, from our work—to go beyond the encouraged mediocrity of our society. It is not about demanding the impossible, but a question of how acutely and fully we can feel in the doing. For once we know the extent of our capability of feeling that sense of satisfaction, fullness, completion, we can then observe which of the various life endeavors brings us closest to that fullness.

—*Audre Lorde*

From *Uses of the Erotic: the Erotic as Power*
originally published in 1978 as *Out & Out Pamphlet #3*, sold for $1.80 at Bloodroot.

Editor's Introduction 7

I FIRST WENT TO BLOODROOT AT AGE 16.

It was 1993 in Southwestern Connecticut, and I was an idealistic teenager growing up in a certain type of Fairfield County neighborhood: tennis, horses, minimum 2-acre zoning requirement. I was sheltered, pained by the world's injustices, and rankled by what I perceived as the continuous moral failings of *other* people. *Most* people, I felt. Sexists, racists, homophobes, non-feminists, meat eaters, mean people, complacent people, boring people, practitioners of violent sports ... potential offenses were legion. Most of my classmates found me equally insufferable.

Fortunately my high school Ethics teacher, Sarah Dubitsky, was sympathetic toward self-righteous naïveté. She could tell I needed to see how principles could prompt productive action. "You must go to Bloodroot," she said after class one day. "It's a feminist vegetarian restaurant and bookstore in Bridgeport. You'll love it." The next weekend my obliging mother drove the 30 miles up the coast.

Ah, Bloodroot! Here were women who framed their lives by their beliefs—through reading, writing, cooking, gardening, handcrafts, publishing, and nourishing their community, literally. As an insatiable reader, an earnest student, a nascent zine publisher, a self-taught vegetarian cook, a novice knitter of awkward acrylic hats: it seemed to me that the women of Bloodroot had invented an ideal life for themselves, sustained it by sharing it with others, and through this, sustained themselves. Bloodroot was—and remains still—an example of how to live and work consciously and conscientiously.

Of course at 16 I was too shy to tell them any of this. How Bloodroot expanded my sense of what was possible, and how its existence filled me with courage and hope. And? It maybe made me kinder. Finally I became aware of dormant potential in my vague feelings.

A decade and a half later, living in Bridgeport, I returned to Bloodroot to take a Sunday weaving class. Reminded of the significance of my teenaged discovery, I began to think about how to share Bloodroot with others. Regardless of the specifics of our politics (which may or may not differ from those outlined in this book), many of us are starved for examples of how to live, everyday, in accordance with our values. We are searching for ways we can better sustain ourselves and our beliefs, and better support each other. Bloodroot, for over 40 years, shows us one such way.

In solidarity—

Emily Larned

Bloodroot in 1980, clockwise from left: Noel Furie, Pat Shea, Selma Miriam, (seated) Betsey Beaven.

BLOODROOT CHRONOLOGY

1975–76	Selma Miriam begins Bloodroot as a weekly feminist cooperative exchange in her home.
1977	Bloodroot Feminist Restaurant & Bookstore opens in March, at 85 Ferris St in Bridgeport CT. The first members of the Bloodroot feminist work collective are Selma Miriam, Samn Stockwell, & Betsey Beaven. Samn Stockwell leaves later that year; Pat Shea & Noel Furie (both original part-time workers) join the collective.
1980	Bloodroot, as Sanguinaria Publishing, publishes their first cookbook, *The Political Palate*.
1984	Pat Shea leaves the collective. Bloodroot, as Sanguinaria Publishing, publishes their next cookbook, *The Second Seasonal Political Palate*.
1987	Liz Seaborn (formerly part-time) joins the collective.
1991	Liz Seaborn leaves the collective.
1993	Sanguinaria publishes *The Perennial Political Palate*.
1997	Sanguinaria publishes *The Addendum to the Political Palate Series*.
2001	Betsey Beaven leaves the collective.
2007	Selma Miriam & Noel Furie as Anomaly Press publish *The Best of Bloodroot*, a two-volume cookbook.
2010	Yale University Library acquires Bloodroot's papers, which are held within Manuscripts & Archives.
2017	Handmade edition of this book is first published by Alder & Frankia, sells out within 9 months.
2018	2nd printing of this book. Anomaly Press publishes *The Bloodroot Calendar Cookbook: New Vegan Recipes*.
2019	Douglas Tirola's documentary *Bloodroot* premieres at the San Francisco Film Festival.

Building Bloodroot

Building Bloodroot 11

Bloodroot: Brewing Visions

1988

This essay was originally published in **Lesbian Ethics** Vol. 3 No. 1 (Albuquerque, NM, edited by Jeanette Silveira). An earlier version had been presented at the W.I.T.C.H. Conference in Boston, MA in 1987. Written in the first person by Selma and Noel a decade after the founding of Bloodroot, this essay chronicles some of the struggles of those early days.

From the Best of Bloodroot Volume 1 (Anomaly Press, 2007, page viii):

"It seems presumptuous to try to summarize second wave feminism, so we will simply say that this is how *we* experienced it. The 1960s were a time of great change. There was the shameful Vietnam War debacle, but there was also the Civil Rights movement. Black and white activism predated feminism and made us as women optimistic about change and the possibility that ordinary folk could make a difference in the world. One of the tools we used was consciousness raising, a technique developed by Paolo Freire, a liberation theologist in South America.

At the time we were angry, but we had great hope. Much feminist work was being written. Hundreds of woman's bookstores sprouted in the late seventies. Ours was unusual in that we combined a bookstore and a restaurant. What did we expect? At least more women in all walks of life previously reserved for men, but much more. We wanted more women doctors, but we wanted a different health care system—more women lawyers and legislators, but also a legal system which took into account women's child care needs and recognized rape and abuse. Ecology was a new word and a new movement. Of course it was feminist to embrace it. Traditional religions teach the inferiority of women and so there was a need for "women's spirituality." We required a recognition that the "patriarchy" was harmful to women (and other living things). We didn't want a piece of the pie; we wanted a new recipe altogether."

SELMA: In trying for perspective on Bloodroot's history, I'm going to write of the Presence of Absence, the image of the Fool in the Tarot, and finally, about being judgmental or, as women say pejoratively, politically correct.

We've been doing Bloodroot, a feminist restaurant and bookstore, for eleven years. Before that, for a year and a half, I did a Wednesday women's night[1] that I called Bloodroot in my home. Before that, there was a rather small conference in Pennsylvania called a National Radical Feminist Conference, intended to discuss how to make feminist communities. And before that, I was married, for a total of 19 years, with two children.

You may remember how it was in the early '70s. Feminists were really angry. We thought that we'd suddenly discovered something that we'd explain to men and everything would change. In 1975, at the National Radical Feminist Conference, Sagaris, a feminist university that had occurred earlier that summer, was criticized at length—for the poor daycare, for taking money from *Ms.* (was Gloria Steinem a CIA dupe?), etc. We assumed that there was a politically appropriate way to function, and we wanted to do it right! One night at this week-

1. Wednesday night continues to be women's night at Bloodroot. Since it is illegal to prevent men from coming, but not illegal to require reservations on the night we have a large group meeting, Wednesday has been women's night every week but two, for eleven years.

Women's night ceased in the early 1990s.
—Selma, 2017.

Selma at the front desk.

long conference, we divided the room into those who would make community on the land and those who would do it in the cities. I sat in the middle, in neither group, unable to think of leaving my friends or home in suburbia.

    I was uncertain about what I wanted to do with my life. I had a lot of fantasies, no sense of what was really possible . . . I was 40 years old, and unhappy—not quite ready to give up my unsatisfactory marriage. Finally, in October 1975, my husband and I decided to separate. He got an apartment in New York City and was to leave by November 1. For three weeks I was frightened and confused, really terrified. He left on a Sunday. The next day, Monday morning, I was driving east for a doctor's appointment. I saw the sun coming up ahead of me, and I knew in a rush what to do. Once a week on Wednesday night, in my own house, I would cook supper. A friend could sell non-sexist books for kids. A photographer would show her work. It would be a women's cooperative exchange and we'd call it Bloodroot. And so we did, for a year and a half. It was fun, but scarcely serious. I continued to worry over the real future, because how could you change your life and the world in suburbia?

    Early the next year a faltering relationship with a woman lover came to an end and there were, one night, strange dreams—of making a garden by Long Island Sound, of rooms of people eating Sunday brunch, of statistics on the dependency of women after divorce that made me cry. In the morning I wrote the dreams down, though I did that rarely, and forgot them. Later that day, I got the same kind of rush I'd had driving east, nine months earlier. I suddenly knew exactly what I wanted to do: make Bloodroot a full time part of my life. Ask other lesbians to do it with me. Use the money I had earned doing landscape design (and had hoarded separate from my husband's and my joint account) for a restaurant and bookstore.

We started looking for a spot. It wasn't until many months later—after we'd rejected the existing diners realtors showed us and the bleak storefronts on the Post Road, and when we'd decided, emotionally, on a building on an inlet of Long Island Sound on a dead end street(no walk-in trade there!) with room for a garden and a terrace—that I then looked back into my journal and found the record of the dreams which seemed to predict just such a place, just such a decision.

Those of you who have read Mary Daly's *Pure Lust* will be familiar with her concept of the Presence of Absence.[2] At that time, I was unable to let my intuition, my third eye function until I was rid of what was truly emotionally disabling—the marriage, and later, the draining relationship. I had been searching, but had no clarity about how to proceed with my life until there was relief from this Presence of Absence, this busy-ness that took from me. I can't help but think this happens often. Women don't know what to do. Our lives are filled with time consuming matters—school, career, jobs, or some relationships that function like television. They waste our time. They waste us. We look for the occasional good program and never know what to do with our Selves.

While we were still doing the cooperative exchange, Jean and Ruth Mountaingrove of *WomanSpirit* magazine came to visit. By then we knew our plans, and so we asked them to do an I Ching about Bloodroot. We cut bamboo that I had planted in my yard, to do the reading in the old yarrow-stalk manner. What we got was hexagram number 4, Youthful Folly—an image of a spring which wells up at the foot of the mountain. And many times, in that period, I would find the Fool in my Tarot readings.

These eleven years seem a state of journeying, of wanting and dreaming, with potential for danger as well as cause for optimism. Like the Fool in the Tarot, we are searchers, traveling our journey. We

---

2. "Male-centered myths and ideologies . . . is 'stuff' that packs the mind, which becomes a garbage heap of details without focus. The glut of non-sense can be experienced watching television, reading newspapers, or attending an ordinary university." **Mary Daly**, ***Pure Lust*** (Boston: Beacon Press, 1984), p. 147. In ***Gyn/Ecology*** (Boston: Beacon Press, 1978), Daly develops the idea of Self (as opposed to self) as an en-spiriting process. See p. 338.

Bloodroot
85 Ferris Street, Bridgeport CT, 06605

haven't stopped. Full of hope, often naive, we believe in the future, and its possibilities. That's what I think Bloodroot is about.

For example, we did (and do) believe in collectivity, even though we didn't know what that meant or how it would work. We did know we didn't want to be bosses with employees. Still, there weren't enough of us to do it all, and some women, both lesbian and straight, wanted to work with us, though not full-time. Since we strongly believe that those fully responsible must be lesbians working full-time with a long term commitment to Bloodroot, we have the collective, and we have the part-time workers. The part time-women, heterosexual and lesbian, give similar reasons for being with us that many of our regular customers give for coming as often as they do. We are different from what is out there, so we are a haven, also a place to think, where they like the ambiance. Recent and current part-timers include a realtor, a drop out from IBM, a massage therapist, a teaching administrator, and a woman who writes and works in book distribution.

As for the collective: well, we started with three. Two came to work part-time but wanted to be with us full-time. First one joined; then one of the originals left, then the other joined. So, in the first two years we became four and it was like that for six years. In that period (just as now) we thought a lot about living our ideals. We found a lesbian lawyer who wanted to help us make our financial arrangement reflect as much as possible what we believed in.[3] As we began to work together, we found that while we all shared responsibility for the business (roughly 60 hours of concentrated attention per week for each of us), we each took specific jobs to do, picking what we felt most comfortable with or what we most wanted to learn.

But after six years one of the four left. And we were still, I think, naive—youthful folly! We couldn't understand why she was restless; we tried to keep

3. The attorney borrowed from a stock agreement **New Words Bookstore** had designed and which came to us by way of one of the original owners of **Womanbooks**. It provided an easy way for those who had not contributed initial capital to buy equivalent amounts of stock. We also decided that while each of us in the collective owns Bloodroot equally, because we want the future of Bloodroot to be secure, the stock cannot appreciate. And so whoever might leave can take with her only her stock value (no more than $1200). She also must sell the stock back to those who stay. Since the value of the stock is low, any lesbian could become a collective member if she desires and if the rest unanimously want her.

her with us, and it was several years of tearing our roots, and several years after that of healing. We tried to write about it in our second cookbook, *The Second Seasonal Political Palate*[4] but it was hard then, in 1984, since it was still so fresh. And so for three years we were three. Then, last year [1987] to our surprise, Liz, one of our part time women, asked to join as a collective member. And as the three of us each privately thought about this, we each separately did our Tarots, and we each got the Fool again. No surprise in that. And so again now, we are four.

Hopeful, like the Fool, we did (and do) hunger to be politically correct. We've wanted to see our lives in a political context, to think what a *feminist* business would be. We thought of the food. I had liked cooking, it was my housewife learned skills—well what was feminist food? And the answer was, ethical and ethnic, vegetarian food, so that people won't starve and animals aren't killed. Ethnic because of all the rich cultures we can explore and all the possibilities that foods present when there is no meat. When the center of a dinner is meat, the same dynamic takes place as when women are focused on men. You know the worry: you can't cut all the good men out of your life, can you? If you're a separatist you try, and what you discover are all the wonderful women/lesbian possibilities—ideas, art, ways of thinking, the way women are different when no men are there—how present we become to ourselves and each other.[5] When meat isn't the center of your dinner, then the possibilities of other foods become endless and much more interesting. Men and meat are types of Presence of Absence. Meat centered dinners are boring.

So we would make space to eat and chat, and of course there had to be books for the ideas we hunger for, and want to talk about. Those books would be the ones we love, or at least like. We're here twelve hours a day, so of course we won't have books we're offended by, or ashamed of. It's our home, after all!

4. **Bloodroot Collective**, *The Second Seasonal Political Palate* (Bridgeport CT; Sanguinaria Publications, 1984) and *The Political Palate*, 1980, are two collections of our recipes flavored with our politics and with quotes from our favorite writers and musicians.

5. **Mary Daly** introduced the idea of women being present to each other in this way in **Beyond God the Father** (Boston, Beacon Press, 1973).

Selma & part-time worker Robin Baena in the kitchen.

And music. We play women's music, 99% lesbian. We believe in its subliminal messages. We have one long wall, opposite the wall of windows that look at the water, that we've filled with old photos of women. We needed to make Bloodroot into a space that is good for us. You can see into the kitchen, and there's no waitressing.

In our "Youthful Folly" we had to be true to ourselves and our vision. We had to be strong in the face of nitpickers. You know how it is in our communities when someone tries to do something? Women, dykes(!) tell you you're serving the wrong brand of beer (meaning Bud instead of Miller) or that the waste basket is in the wrong place or that your salads are more expensive than at another restaurant (ignoring that your soups are cheaper). You can imagine that to the Fool this kind of carping was dismaying.

And other painful stumbles the Fool made? Well, many. I wish we hadn't fallen in love so often with women we wished would stay with us. But that's ridiculous; sharing good work with someone makes you love her. It's as if there has been a love affair with Bloodroot and with us, and just as is often true in love affairs, there is the exciting beginning when all one's hungry needs seem to be met. Then difficult reality sets in when differences become apparent, and it is necessary to *want* to make it work, to realize that when you are not distanced from your work and those who work with you, struggle is required. I think it is the same in lover relationships. Lesbians are so much like each other, so we come closer in our intimacy. Too often we have seen lesbians settling for other ways to think than lesbian feminism. Apolitical health concerns such as obsessions with food allergies or macrobiotics[6] become the focus of their lives. Then there are women whose lovers want to exclude what is politically challenging in favor of a more "normal" life, and there are those who leave because they need a "real" job, as if we were a fantasy. There were times when there were precious few

6. Traditional Japanese food, with its balance of salty, pickled, and bland whole grain is as useful for vegetarian inspiration and modification as are other cuisines of the Far East—Chinese, Indian, Thai, etc. The *conceptions* of macrobiotics, however, are woman hating and homophobic. For example, in the June '87 issue of **Macrobiotics Today**, **Lima Ohsawa** is reported to have apologized for her husband's dying. It is explained that she and he are one. In other issues, such as January '86, female homosexuality and independence are blamed for sickness. I will also argue that the macrobiotic advised exclusion of the nightshade family (peppers, eggplants, tomatoes, and potatoes) is hard to justify for Native Americans, since most of these plants are "new" world in origin, never mind for the Italians, Irish, Spanish, etc.

of us struggling to get the work done so that Bloodroot would survive.

The other big disappointment is the lack of recognition we've had from lesbian and feminist media. (It is interesting that the animal rights movement, which is as fraught with factions and arguments as is our own, has been so repeatedly admiring of us, not only bringing us customers, but making us feel valued in what we do!) For the past eleven years we have been a visible feminist and known lesbian presence in a blue collar residential neighborhood in one of the largest and poorest cities in the Northeast. All of our printed materials and the sign over the door carry the word feminist. Above the counter (where food is picked up by customers) are feminist and animal rights cartoons and occasional clippings of interest to us. We led a neighborhood fight against a recreational developer who wanted the city to take the waterfront land we owned away from us by eminent domain, and we received overwhelming support from our neighbors, who see us as hard working "girls" who are quiet and grow flowers. In the lesbian section of our bookstore we have a sign that says *"Gentlemen—We trust those of you who support women's self determination will curb your curiosity about lesbian books and limit your browsing to other sections of the store. Thank you."*

Our clientele is surprisingly mixed, as out-of-state dykes often comment. Folks come from the rich suburbs of Westport, poor neighborhoods in Bridgeport (knowing there's good homemade bread and soup, cheap, here), and from the women's community in New Haven, a half-hour away. The lesbians and gay men who come in know what we're about. The straight women see us working together, often laughing and playing around, sometimes angry or downhearted. We are a visible example of what can be done without men. Of course they come to us and expect us to commiserate when they are in crisis or to celebrate when they win one against the patriarchy. It is clear to anyone who wants to notice that we are lesbian separatists, functioning right here out in the world, running what *Vegetarian Times* has called one of the best (Mariclare Barrett Orbis' favorite) vegetarian restaurants in the country.[7]

So perhaps you can imagine that the overwhelming silence on the part of the lesbian press has been a disappointment,[8] and the occasional pot shot or snide remark exceedingly painful. It seems we were naïve to think our own papers would be as encouraged by our existence as we have been by theirs.

The Fool has had good discoveries also. We have found that when you have a vision and you try to be true to it, to go on thinking, working, talking, you do become stronger and more intuitive in the way you make judgments. We often were surprised that we had each, separately, come to the same conclusion. We could *see* courage, as we looked out from our kitchen.

We are fortunate to have been able to create a life that is relatively integrated. We don't work at a job, go home to leisure time when one might cook or eat or go to a movie, and then wait for a vacation, or a date on the weekend. Instead, we have our daily work that we do together, talking, laughing, sometimes fighting. We cook the food and serve it together and at least go home with our books, read for a while and then sleep. In the morning some more reading and then back to work, to talk about what we've read. These Winter days, when business is slower, we'll sit and knit. In the Spring, we'll start the garden. Every few weeks, our menu changes, partly to reflect changing food availability, partly because we'd be bored doing it the same all the time. This rhythm to our lives, this working hard, is tiring, but not boring! And of course, there are the customers, many of whom have become our friends. It's not that we don't take vacations. We have for the past 7 or 8 years. But our daily lives *have* to be a satisfaction in themselves, for us to continue, as we do.

7. **Mariclare Barrett Orbis**, Food Editor, *Vegetarian Times*, March '85: "This is the high water mark for fine vegetarian cuisine... Bloodroot is, in fact, my favorite US vegetarian restaurant." And March '87: "Vegetarian and feminist ethics share a consciousness of our connections with other species and with the survival of the Earth. The women of the Bloodroot Collective cherish the act of creating—with the Earth and with each other."

8. With notable exceptions, such as **Lee Lanning** in *Maize*, **Batya Bauman** who wrote to *WomaNews* about us, and **Carol Seajay** in *Feminist Bookstore News.*

Noel.

In this context, questions such as "Are you for censorship or freedom of speech?" have no meaning. What kind of boredom is there in lesbian lives to produce a market for *On Our Backs*, or for the violent, racist emanations from Lace Publications?[9]

Those of us who call ourselves feminist make our Selves and other women a priority. We are angry and political; we make judgments for our Selves. Lesbians discuss substance abuse, work towards "survival" of alcoholism, incest, patriarchal religion; yet some don't seem to recognize that sadomasochism is our own internalization of men's woman-hating. Sure, drugs, alcohol, religions (including those such as macrobiotics) are all turn-ons, ways to lose one's mind, one's Self. And so is the self-hatred in the so-called "freedom" of whips and bondage.

As you can see, we are proud to make judgments. Of course we want to live in a way that is healing, and exciting. Of course we want to be in possession of our Selves, even while we know we need encouragement from each other. We are passionate about our lives, we want to be engaged, on our journey, proceeding sometimes naively and always opinionated.

NOEL: When I was a little girl I formed images of how I wanted to be in the world. I imagined myself proud, self-sufficient, strong and free. The picture which always came to mind as a symbol was a straight spine, head held high. Between that time 37 years ago when I was six years old and now (I'm 43), much has happened to pull me away from the vision and back again. I now think of this journey as a spiral.

In *Right-Wing Women*[10] Andrea Dworkin talks about patriarchy's[11] brothel and farm models for womanhood. Before I came out, and before I came to Bloodroot, I had been both. Neither worked for me then any more than the lesbian versions (sadomasochism and having babies) would work for me today.

9. **Lace Publications** was apparently created so that **Artemis Oakgrove** could write about "dominating dykes, sex slaves… and sumptuous living… raw sex… dominion and dependency," to quote from their February '88 brochure.

10. Andrea Dworkin, *Right Wing Women* (New York, Putnam, 1983). See pp. 174–193 for Andrea's thorough discussion of these concepts.

11. I use the term patriarchy throughout this piece because it is the only word I know which describes the totality of men's ownership of this world we try to live in. Patriarchy is the rule of the fathers; it is the process and the end result of male destruction of life.

Selma Miriam, President, and Noel Furie, Vice President, in a newspaper photograph of the Westport Weston National Organization of Women (NOW) chapter, 1974.

In an attempt to fit into the brothel model (the only option I could envision at the time) I was a fashion model from the age of 13 until I was 18. I then began to work as a Playboy Bunny in New York. Those two occupations amounted to the same thing—selling flesh. After about a year and a half (during which time I was acutely aware of the humiliation I felt), I decided to try what I now think of as the farm model. Because I believed I would find some pride in a more socially acceptable role, I became a wife, the mother of two children (they are 16 and 18 now), the owner of one dog, one cat and a house in suburbia. By then I was in my mid 30s and crazy to find something of meaning in my life. My childhood image of strength had become a very dim memory.

At this point Selma and Betsey came into my life. (I seduced them both at various times!) I met Selma through NOW and a consciousness-raising group. She and Betsey, and then later Patty, lived together. Both of them were looking for ways to live their lives as radical lesbians. I was in the emotional upheaval of coming out, of not knowing what my life could possibly become, when I began to work part-time at Bloodroot. (Patty, later to be a collective member also, began at about the same time.)

Those early years working at Bloodroot were extremely difficult for me. I struggled to juggle: taking care of young children and of my emotions (which were wild), and learning how to work the long hard hours required at Bloodroot with other lesbians in very close proximity physically, emotionally, and psychically. I wonder now what it was that I knew then that kept me there through those hard early years, as I had no language for what was happening.

After a period of time, language began to form and it became clear that I wanted to make Bloodroot my life, that collectivity in our work and living arrangements was a real possibility, and that I needed to think of lesbian relationships, our relationships, in a new way. During this period, my childhood image of the straight spine returned in a form I now call stamina.

Stamina (from the Latin root *stare*: to stand) means the fixed, firm part of a body which supports it or gives it strength. In other words, the backbone. And it also means endurance and staying power.[12] The existence of Bloodroot opened up the possibility of living my life by radical lesbian values—values I was discovering were my own. My desire for a life of pride and meaning re-awakened the image of the straight spine, and Bloodroot became the way in which I might work toward it. I believed that if I endured, had the staying power so to speak, in the end I would have the life that I passionately wanted, and needed in order to survive. I would have something which was not an imitation of heterosexual society (neither brothel nor farm), but something which would be truly radical and in which I could begin to form and live my dreams.

One implication of the word stamina is that if we have it, we stand on our own; we are not dependent

12. I want to thank **Mary Daly** for her investigation into the roots of words. She has inspired me to do the same.

Betsey Beaven, Pat Shea, Noel Furie, Barbara Beckelman, Selma Miriam.

13. **Sarah Hoagland** discussed her yet-to-be published book ***Lesbian Ethics*** at Bloodroot in February 1988. (She expects to have the book

on one another for our Selves. This isn't easy given our hungers and the damage that has been done to all of us by patriarchy. But I know from my own experience that stamina is essential for us at Bloodroot, as I believe it is for all radical lesbian feminists. And I also know that the forms of relationship which encourage dependency erode the possibility for stamina and the creativity born of it. I believe we need *every bit* of that creativity to make our revolution and our world.

Bloodroot functions collectively—that is, we are inter-dependent. I have come to see our inter-dependence as valuable, radical, and different from dependence.[13] We each have individual strengths and skills to put toward the making of the whole.

It goes something like this: one of us creates new recipes, another can tell what spice will make the soup perfect, another builds and fixes things, another is patient with sauces that cook slowly, and so on. These functions overlap, of course, as do others, but it seems that each of us ends up doing what we like and/or do best. All of us and our skills are what Bloodroot is. As a matter of fact, *Bloodroot* was chosen as our name because, among other things, each flower and each leaf of this plant grow separately from the others. But the leaves touch and the roots are interconnected as can be seen in our drawing. We see ourselves this way—individual yet interconnected. (And Bloodroot makes for a nice prolific patch in the garden, too!)

out by Halloween 1988.) In the course of that talk she differentiated between being "dependent" and "depending upon." This clarification was important to me because our interdependency requires that we depend upon one another in tangible work-related ways as well as in intangible ways.

Collective member Liz Seaborn.

IN 1984, AFTER SIX YEARS in the collective, Patty came to the decision that she had to leave. Because of the intimate manner in which we had all been connected, pulling out her roots all tangled up with ours was exceedingly painful.[14] She had been a lover, friend and partner and had lived with Selma and Betsey for six years. During that period, in 1980, I had bought my house together with another woman who worked part-time at Bloodroot. We all comprised, for want of a better word, a family. Our connections were defined in many ways, sometimes sexual, but not always. I loved the woman with whom I had bought my house. Although we were not lovers, certainly there were emotional ties of great depth. Ties to Selma and Patty, as well as to Betsey and my housemate, were strong and deep. Patty's going and the departure of other women who have worked with us over the years, including my housemate, require us to consider their reasons.

I think there are many. The work at Bloodroot is enormously demanding physically. And it does not pay well according to the standards of the patriarchy out there. What we, that is Selma, Betsey, myself, and now Liz, our new collective member, derive from our work here apparently is not valued enough by these women to compensate for the struggle required. Sometimes I think the rewards we reap can't even be imagined. There have been times when the intimacy and intensity of work in our kitchen, with all its internal and external pressure, is more difficult than some women can or wish to cope with.

Lesbians often assume that it is simple to work together—and then they come here to discover that it is maybe the hardest thing they have ever done. Some lesbians leave Bloodroot for the protection and security of a couple arrangement. We have found that the lesbian who is outside Bloodroot is often jealous of the time and energy her lover must put and/or wants to put into Bloodroot. In *Gyn/Ecology* Mary Daly states: " the courage to stand/move

14. After Patty left, I wrote a fable to explain to myself and to others who might be interested, why it was she left and what, in very simple terms, it meant to us all. The fable is in Spanish because I found a different and fresh imagination there. We printed it in the ***Second Seasonal Political Palate*** (1984).

alone ... is at the heart of the courage to bond."[15]
I believe Mary is speaking of the radical bonding we work toward. Some forms of coupleness obviate the possibility of commitment to Bloodroot because it is impossible to bond with us and fill the demands of the relationship at the same time. In many ways it is also easier to be in a relationship of dependency than to have community with us and the struggle that entails.

There are other reasons too. But I believe the core of it is not *wanting enough*: the daily connection with other lesbians that Bloodroot affords, the real separation from the patriarchy that is our lives, and the resulting Selves that we are Becoming.

The patriarchy wants women weak, separated from each other, self-abusive, locked into dependent relationships, and predictable in our destruction of each other and our Selves. It wants to destroy courage in us so that even the imagining of a lesbian feminist world is impossible. And patriarchy has many weapons toward the destruction of our courage, including television and the rest of the media, religion, therapy, motherhood, "free speech," and the farm and brothel models (presented as our only options for existence as lesbians or as straight women).

Here at Bloodroot we've been together for eleven years in a space that is, to a large extent, separate from the patriarchy and from which we can keep a subjective beady eye on all its doings. And here I've learned to return to that early vision of myself and to value the stamina and radical courage we are growing. We use both stamina and the collective strength we derive from our radical lesbian bonding to persist in our rebellion. ✹

---

[15]. Mary Daly, *Gyn/Ecology: The Metaethics of Radical Feminism* (Boston: Beacon Press, 1978), p. 345.

Selma, Noel, and Barbara Beckelman in the kitchen. Unidentified customers in the foreground.

The Political Palate

1980

The Political Palate was the first cookbook published by the Bloodroot Collective. While consisting mostly of recipes, each volume is prefaced by essays, seasoned throughout with quotes from the members' favorite books, and supplemented by a bibliography of feminist material. It is truly a cookbook for and by readers.

In a 2012 post to her blog (www.selmaslist.blogspot.com, February 3), *Selma elaborates on how Bloodroot became vegetarian.*

"Two friends in our local NOW chapter, **Priscilla Feral** (who later became head of Friends of Animals) and **Jim Mason**, co-author with **Peter Singer** of *Animal Factories*, urged me to make the food served in the restaurant vegetarian. So we did ... not out of a heart-felt commitment, but being convinced intellectually that it was right ... But as we went on, that initial commitment became the core of our beliefs.

Jim went on to work on his book, *An Unnatural Order.* He did an enormous amount of research on pre-agricultural humans, and how agriculture and animal husbandry changed human character and health. And how together with the monotheistic religions, a ladder of privilege was established (in contrast to animism and female fertility religions). The result was layers of contempt for those below god and man: meaning women, people who were different (in color), animals and the earth itself. In Jim's book, we gradually come to understand that stewardship, the shepherd caring for his flock, is a euphemism for the right to construct and shape other creatures and humans to the particular forms and beliefs of a dominant culture. These beliefs went on to enable sexual engineering, slavery and genocide. Jim met with us periodically as he was writing his book, and what was most impressive was that he always listened, as few men do.

There have been many books since *An Unnatural Order* was published—books about the environment and animal rights, but no book I know of has such depth and breadth, and is at the same time feminist in its perspective, and in its condemnation of a dominionist mind set."

Introduction

WHAT IS A FEMINIST COOKBOOK? What's a feminist restaurant? There's no such thing as feminist food! So people have said.

This is what we say: We are feminists, that is we recognize that women are oppressed by patriarchy—the rule of the fathers—and we commit ourselves to rebellion against that oppression. Feminism is not a part-time attitude for us; it is how we live all day, everyday. Our choices in furniture, pictures, the music we play, the books we sell, and the food we cook all reflect and express our feminism. Our food is vegetarian because we are feminists. We are opposed to the exploitation, domination, and destruction which come from factory farming and the hunter with the gun. We oppose the keeping and killing of animals for the pleasure of the palate just as we oppose men controlling abortion or sterilization. We won't be part of the torture and killing of animals.[1] We know that humans, being omnivores, can live quite well without meat and that there is much evidence (the length of our intestines, the number of molars for grinding) to indicate that our bodies are best designed for the consumption of grains and vegetables. Meat eating can be justified in an environment that produces no other foods.[2] We are less

1. *Woman's Creation* by **Elizabeth Fisher** examines in depth the connections between oppression of animals and of women. For example, "the sexual subjugation of women, as it is practiced in all the known civilizations of the world, was modeled after the domestication of animals. The domestication of women followed long after the initiation of animal keeping, and it was then that men began to control women's reproductive capacity, enforcing chastity and sexual repression... Animals, on the other hand, may well have been the earliest form of private property on any considerable scale, making animal domestication the pivot also in the development of class differences." p. 190 (Anchor-Doubleday, Garden City, NY, & McGraw-Hill Paperback, 1980). Also see **Singer, Peter,** *Animal Liberation: a New Ethics For a Treatment of Animals* (Avon Press, NYC, NY, 1975); and **Mason, Jim, & Singer, Peter,** *Animal Factories* (Crown Publishers, NYC, NY, 1980). Both discuss vegetarianism from an ethical, that is, a political point of view.

exclusionary of fish and do sometimes serve it at our restaurant.³ Since, however, we wanted to prove how well people can eat on a vegetarian diet, we have included only eight recipes in this book which use fish.

Feminist food is seasonal. We use what's close at hand, what is most fresh and local and therefore least expensive and least "preserved." This seems obvious, but we know of no other serious attempt at a seasonal cookbook. Our lives are so disconnected from organic or natural timekeeping and the best efforts of the earth, that once we enter the sterile world of pre-packaged supermarkets it is hard to remember that strawberries and tomatoes are not worth eating in January and that onion soup and oranges don't make sense in August.

To us, being feminists or woman-oriented means celebrating holidays which predate Judaism and Christianity. The solstices and equinoxes are closer to the earth's rhythms, and celebrating the waning and growing light, seeds sprouting or the harvest brought in, makes more sense than the obscenity of noise and false jollity that is Christmas/New Years, or the celebration of masochism/martyrdom that is Easter. Despite the rationalization that these holidays derive from earlier pagan cultures, their continued observation in a Christian context is an endorsement of a theology and value system which continues opposition to abortion and the ERA, believes homosexuality to be a sin or disease, and confuses masochism and eroticism. We believe that carrying on "holiday" traditions of a system which is, *per se*, anti-woman, is concretely harmful to our minds and spirits. So we don't take note of these holidays. Instead this book is divided by solstices and equinoxes and by the cross-quarter days which would fall between, making eight break points in the year. While the Celtic calendar is one form of time-reckoning feminists might use and the ever-changing thirteen-month lunar calendar is another, both are simply examples of what nature oriented calendars might be like.⁴ We wanted

---

2. "While humans are and always have been omnivorous, during the major part of our evolution, as in most parts of the earth even today, vegetables provided most of our sustenance, a fact which is reflected in our eight-yard-long gut, the shape and surface of our teeth, possibly in the fact that animal fats seem to contribute to hardening of the arteries and that most of the known long-lived peoples—the Hunzas, the Abkhazians, and the Ecuadorians—eat very little meat." pp. 57–58, **Woman's Creation** by **Elizabeth Fisher**, op. cit.

3. *Bloodroot stopped serving fish in 1980.* —Selma, 2017.

4. Sample calendars include **Sister Heathenspinster's** *Lunation Calendar* from 809 Maggard Iowa City, IA 52240, and *The Lunar Calendar* from Luna Press, Box 511, Kenmore Square, Boston, MA 62215. Be sure to see **Moon, Moon** by **Rush, Anne Kent** (Moon Books, P.O. Box 9223, Berkeley, CA 94709) for a fine chapter on timekeeping.

Bloodroot dolls, handmade by Selma.

to stay with what is familiar to all of us while indicating the earth's rhythms by our time divisions.

Feminist food, in our case, is produced by a collective. That means each of us does what she can do best and that we learn from and teach each other. It means that, because we are working at what we want to be doing (which is to make a women's space, informed by women's values), we care very much about what we produce. Our food is our art. That means we are very particular, that continuity is important to us, that we all taste and discuss the final seasoning of a soup. It means we admire the simplicity of quick breads, puddings, or boiled greens and that we also appreciate the richness of a quiche or the elegance of an endive salad.

Because we think of cooking as an art form, some discussion of our thoughts concerning the connection of art and politics is necessary. We all are taught that art is special, beyond our daily lives, requiring the learning of an obscure code of communication taught by experts. Since both those experts and the artists themselves share the general misogyny of society[5] and the work of women artists has been ignored (as documented by Harris and Nochlin, Judy Chicago, Lucy Lippard, Eleanor Tufts, Germaine Greer[6]) a woman aspiring to learn how to make aesthetic judgments acquires an expertise that is irrelevant or negative regarding women's daily lives. Meanwhile other "lower" art forms bombard us with the violence of pornography and punk

5. See **Chicago, Judy,** *Through the Flower* (Doubleday, Garden City, NY 1975) p. 156 & p. 164. Also "Retrochic: Looking Back in Anger" by **Lucy Lippard,** *The Village Voice,* December 10, 1979.

6. **Harris & Nochlin,** *Women Artists: 1550–1950* (Knopf, NYC, NY, 1976): **Tufts, Eleanor,** *Our Hidden Heritage: Five Centuries of Women Artists* (Paddington Press, NYC, NY,

1974); **Lippard, Lucy**, *From the Center* (Dutton, NYC, NY, 1976); **Chicago, Judy**, *Through the Flower*, op. cit., **Chicago, Judy**, *The Dinner Party* (Doubleday, Garden City, NY, 1979); and **Greer, Germaine**, *The Obstacle Race: The Fortunes of Women Painters and Their Work* (Farrar, Straus and Giroux, NYC, NY, 1979).

7. "Retrochic: Looking Back In Anger" by **Lucy Lippard**, cited above, is a discussion of current art as political expression.

8. See **Lerner, Gerda**, *The Majority Finds Its Past: Placing Women in History* (Oxford University Press, 1979). **Lerner** argues that women's experiences have been trivialized or deleted from history altogether, since the building of service organizations, the establishment of schools and libraries are deemed less important than waging war and signing treaties. Two quotes: "The central question raised by women's history is: what would history be like if it were seen through the eyes of women and ordered by the values they define?" and "All history as we now know it is, for women, merely prehistory." Also see "Female Support Networks and Political Activism: Lillian Wald, Crystal Eastman, Emma Goldman," by **Blanche Wiesen Cook** in *Chrysalis*, No. 3. **Cook** also edited *Crystal Eastman on Women and*

rock (as rape and wife beating increase), the lies of sentimentality and romanticism, and the excesses of consumerism. "Art" is used as justification for pornography in high fashion magazines or for the latest racism and woman hating in the galleries[7]; the lies of advertising are justified by the dollars they supposedly bring in. Somewhere the two merge and become a perversion we are not supposed to understand or evaluate. Both leave us numb and alienated.

Yet it seems obvious that art is communication about what we experience and what we believe, and is, therefore inherently political. It is effective when it speaks to our real experiences, not to the phony responses we have been taught are appropriate. Working together daily in our own space, we are beginning to trust our intuition and our intelligence as we judge these forms of communication. It is much harder to do this when we are in offices, private homes, supermarkets. Because of the isolation of women in patriarchy, we find it hard to develop women's (feminist) judgment. The best a "liberated" woman can do is to learn their code and "think like a man." When we stop wanting to do that, when we start wanting women's values, women's art and women's politics, then we need new images, new words, new ways to think as Mary Daly, Adrienne Rich and others have written. We need new ways to live. As we and others begin finding these ways, we must remember that women have done this before and that much of the history of it has been ignored, not recorded, or destroyed.[8] We cook as a way to survive economically, yet our cooking is part of our study, our living, and our politics. It seems to us that there is no separation between art and politics; there is integrity which requires judgments and a value system underlying our work and our lives. Everything we do is the result.

Many of our customers assume we are a health food restaurant. We don't think we are, though eating recently at a local hospital cafeteria and noting how oversalted and oversugared the food was (and how replete with additives) made us wonder. Our philosophy is vegetarian and seasonal. Yes, we do use sugar and salt, though a lot less than people are used to. We always have some sugar-free desserts on our menu and you will find both kinds of recipes in this book. We experiment to develop sugar-free, baking powder-free, and low salt dishes. We are extremely interested in soy protein for those who cannot or do not wish to eat dairy products. Much more remains to be done. Because our food must be (taste) wonderful, we make our pie crust of butter and white pastry flour.[9] We make a whole wheat bread but also serve and enjoy other breads made with unbleached white flour in combination with whole grains. We do believe in eating whole grain foods, but in some dishes, white rice tastes better to us, and so that's what we use! You must decide to what degree health considerations enter your cooking.[10]

More on political cooking can be found in William Shurtleff's and Akiko Aoyagi's *Book of Tofu* and *Book of Miso* from Autumn Press and *Book of Tempeh* from Harper & Row. These books are about the misuse of the earth that results in starvation and about cultures whose way of life demand concern with balance and quality instead of the tradition of excess typical in the West. They are well worth reading for data on protein availability, even if you don't want to learn about tofu, miso, or tempeh. They are truly political books in the respect they show for eastern cultures and their desire to appropriately inform us of the value of our own efforts to live responsibly with concern for others.

Our interest in ethnic cooking means we love discovering early New England recipes for "Indian" pudding or for molasses-apple gingerbread. We also hope to

Revolution, (Oxford University Press, 1978). Her study of the women who were responsible for Workers' Compensation Laws, the founding of ACLU and WILPF is fascinating but embittering when we realize how well men such as Eastman's brother Max are remembered while the women are forgotten. More recently the work of Lillian Smith, Rosa Parks, Fannie Lou Hamer in their struggles with racism are being ignored and forgotten while men's names remain in the limelight. See "Pauli Murray" in **Ms. Magazine**, March 1980, to learn that it was a black woman's senior law thesis which was used as the main argument against separate but equal in *Brown vs. Board of Education* and who developed techniques of confidence and self restraint for student protests in the '40s which became the basis of non-violent civil rights action in the '60s.

9. *Though not anymore!* — Selma, 2017

10. See **Dinaberg** & **Akel**, *Nutrition Survival Kit* (Panjandrum Press/Aris Books, San Francisco, CA, 1976) for a sensible and well-written guide to the health aspects of a vegetarian diet.

learn much more about non-meat eating cultures. It seems poor peoples have had intuitive understanding of protein complementarity while caring how to make food taste good. While our heritage means we know most about American, French-Italian ("continental") and eastern European cooking, we want to learn more about Japanese cuisine with its exceptional respect for the seasons and Indian cooking with its exquisitely seasoned vegetarian dishes. We are discovering Middle Eastern lentil and vegetable combinations, Native American cooking, and the use of peanuts and root vegetables in Africa and South America. There is much to learn from other cultures and no need to get confused with other woman-hating systems of thought such as which foods are yin and which yang.

We must remember the continuity of recipes within any given culture. We have experimented and changed to our taste; however, all our recipes derive from others. Many of our favorite dishes came from friends and customers (and they will be duly noted) though we have, at times, made changes in them. Much of our cooking is derived or adapted from what we have learned from the best cookbook authors[11]: Paula Peck, Julia Child, Craig Claiborne, Michael Field, Elizabeth David, and the writers of *Gourmet* magazine and the Time-Life *Foods of the World* series. And some of our best vegetarian soups are from Julie Jordan's *Wings of Life*, (Crossing Press), our favorite vegetarian cookbook. We don't believe in secret recipes. Our file is open to anyone who wants to copy, and we hope we have properly acknowledged where inspiration or recipe has come from.

We must warn you that our recipes assume the use of good equipment and good raw ingredients. We have a restaurant stove, a big Hobart mixer for kneading bread, and a large food processor for making purées. Of course you can use a blender or a sieve and you can knead small quantities of

---

11. See the cookbook bibliography for a list of our favorite cookbooks.

bread by hand, but our recipes assume you will put the extra effort into doing the job adequately. And we believe there is no substitute for sweet butter, good-quality aged soy sauce, fresh herbs in certain dishes, Switzerland Swiss and Italian well-aged Parmesan, or real heavy cream when called for. We don't compromise quality. We hope you don't need to either.

As for counting calories and watching the waistline, we're not interested. Dieting has been an especially oppressive masochism expected of women in recent years. An obsession with slenderizing is supposed to give women the illusion of control over their lives—a rationale expressed by the anorexic as well as implicit in behavior modification or other easy or hard diet regimes. It should be obvious that we come in all sizes, different shapes as well as different heights, and therefore enforced thinness is starvation and misery. It is an illness created by the attitude that the only beautiful or healthy size is thin.[12]

We are writing this "cookbook" for all the people who asked for it. When we began, we had little enthusiasm for the effort until we realized that to "feed" you, we had to tell you what feeds us. Without our best loved treasures—the resources in our bookstore to think about, talk about and try to live by—our long hours of cooking and cleaning are drudgery.[13] The songs, poems, stories and ideas are necessary to our lives; we hope to awaken your interest in them, and that you will pursue them beyond the small tastes we offer here.[14] ✿

12. There is some feminist analysis of food in ***A Woman's Conflict: The Special Relationship Between Women and Food***, by **Jane Rachel Kaplan** (Spectrum, Englewood Cliffs, NJ, 1980), in particular the Introduction, "A Woman's Body in a Man's World," "Working Up an Appetite," & "Farming Out the Home." Be careful of sexist presumptions in some articles, especially the acceptance of **Desmond Morris**' theories in "Venus as Endomorph" and the supposedly funny "Women in the Kitchen: the feminist boiling point."

13. *Now I would say tedious—not drudgery!* —Selma, 2017

14. Also see ***The Fat Illusion*** & ***Fat Liberation —A Luxury?***, both by **Aldebaran** as well as other materials from Fat Liberation Front, P.O. Box 342, New Haven, CT 06513; i.e., ***The Calorie Controversy —Who's Cheating?*** & ***A Fat Women's Problem Solving Group: Radical Change***.

Some Notes on the Passage of the Seasons . . .

PART OF THE NECESSITY OF SURVIVAL is the need to reclaim the natural time-marked events of the earth. As the water in our women's bodies subtly responds to the daily changing high and low tides of the moon, so indeed some part of our spirits respond to the larger changes the seasons bring us. By observing the events of the seasons, the Spring and Fall Equinoxes, Summer and Winter Solstices, and cross quarter days, women can begin to claim their own sense of birth and death. In our need to reevaluate what food to eat or medicine to use, even to learn women's ways of loving, we can consciously try to realign ourselves with the earth's cycles. In this way, we may be able to discover the justice that exists in the real world of nature.

Seasonally a kind of justice takes place. Beginning with what is called witch's new year on October 31 (November eve is a cross quarter day which marks the mid point between Fall Equinox and Winter Solstice), a certain direction is set for us. This cross quarter day gives clear indications that the light and temperature of the earth are changing. In late October, our bodies respond to the smell of decay and the chill of afternoons growing shorter. Our senses act

Some Notes on the Passage of the Seasons

as a guide. As the sun withdraws in early afternoon, this signals our anticipation of withdrawal for the winter as other cross quarter days (February 2, May 1, August 2) mark the anticipation of Spring, Summer, and Fall respectively.

Winter Solstice (December 22) brings us to the "new moon of the sun" or the longest night of the year. It is a time when women particularly need to recognize that the "destructiveness" of what takes place on earth naturally—the newly frozen stilled earth enveloped in darkness—is the opposite of the active evil of nuclear energy and nuclear weapons. While some conscious women struggle to live in the sometimes cold space of our truths underground, a world above ground frantically celebrates the hollow "holidays" of Christmas and New Years.

Spring Equinox (March 21) brings with it the strong winds which remind us that the sun is traveling faster than any other time of year.[1] It is a time to look closely at the earth's beginning growths and to sense that the equality of day and night gives us clues to the earth's secrets of balance.

Summer Solstice comes on June 21 and while the earth is warming with the rays of the sun, we shed our clothing to feel its power more directly. It is a good time to think about the morality of women's love for each other and how the power of that love quickens and moves our lives together.

Fall Equinox (September 21) brings us to the fullness of the harvest which is at one with the culmination of life cycles. To the extent that we can live fulfilling lives, women are reminded that we need to take death and dying into our own hands—that life at any cost is as senseless an act against our natures as any other victimization we might experience ... ☉

---

1. "Storms that arise during an equinox are sometimes called equinoctial gales, for a very good reason. At this time the sun travels north or south faster than at any other time of the year. In a week it moves over 2½°, or half the distance between the two pointers in the Big Dipper. This change in the sun's position produces such variations in the pattern of warm and cold air masses that violent storms are often caused." p. 269, Vol. 6 *The World Book Encyclopedia*, 1969.

The Second Seasonal Political Palate

1984

The Second Political Palate was the second cookbook published by the Bloodroot Collective as Sanguinaria Publishing. Pat (Patty) Shea had left the collective earlier in the year.

Bloodroot's archive at Yale includes many letters from women, many of which echo similar sentiments:

February 9, 1981
"Let me tell you Selma: that spirit of community and love ... [at Bloodroot] is unique and, for me, in this life in male-oriented fields, totally fantasy-ideal—I can hardly even *imagine* it. I know you know how unusual it is; I know you treasure it. I benefit from even *hearing* about it." —A.S.

February 15, 1984
"I am still feeling so high from being with you all. So bizarre to go into work on Monday—it's like I am two womyn —my secret, special, real self lives safe inside while I relate [to others at work] ...
—S.R.

Feminism in the Eighties

FEMINISM PROCEEDS INTO THE EIGHTIES as nuclear proliferation grows, acid rain and general pollution worsen, and the escalation of everyday violence against women and children continues. Everyone we know is frantically trying to see Reagan defeated. Discouragement is rife, and yet there always seems to be hope. Why else would Sonia Johnson run for President? In *WomanSpirit*, Summer 1984, Johnson wrote:

So where can we turn for hope? Being revolutionaries, which we are, means that we're distinguished from the rest of the population by the fact that we have hope. The world, and the Women's Movement right now, is characterized by a very deep despair. We're the ones who are not despairing, and who understand that if we despair, all is lost. There always has to be not just hope, but real honest-to-goodness faith and trust in ourselves, in one another and our ability to make the new world and to make it happen in our lifetime.

Because, another assumption that the System always teaches people is that you can work and work, and maybe some day you can change it. But it won't be in your lifetime. Maybe your children will see it.

Well, who said we couldn't make a difference in our lifetime? It was Them. It was the enemy. Of course we can make a difference! And we must. Because if we don't do it in our lifetime, there won't be any more lifetime for anybody.

We are surprised at the growth in feminist consciousness in many circles, even while we are dismayed at the backlash and at the number of women who give up under the pressures of phallocracy.

When we began Bloodroot in 1977, we were encouraged by the growing women's movement and believed we would be one of many working in that community. We've since discovered that many feminist-oriented businesses started in that year, and many of those are gone now, though new ventures start all the time. There is a difference between community and movement.

Oppressed communities often find themselves bonding in weakness. A feminist *movement*, on the other hand, requires vision and persistence as well as a recognition of the ways patriarchy can divide us. Struggling to remove the embedded self-hate and fragmentation is very difficult indeed. We are more affected by the reactionary politics of the eighties than most of us realize. As the struggle gets harder, success seems that much further off and many women feel "burnt out."

The media has exclaimed that here we are in 1984 and it's not as bad as predicted. It seems worse to us in many ways. What we see, concomitant with growing political conservatism, is encouragement for women to return to make-up and high heels and a romanticizing of childbirth. We see that *The New York Times Magazine* has joined the growing ranks of soft-porn periodicals, and domestic and sexual violence have increased sharply, not only in severity but in propensity. Aren't more and more women suffering from breast and uterine problems unheard of years ago? The forests and lakes are dying. The United States military industrial complex is encouraging the destruction of third world natural resources, and worse, their patterns of survival. A litany of disasters.

Meanwhile here at home, computer literacy is touted as a necessary tool for feminist endeavors. We seem to be unable to learn that technology *per se* is not politically neutral, that the kind of knowledge we need is neither of better bombs nor of better software, that even disregarding physical damage done to women (especially third world) who make or work on computer machinery, communication by machine is not the answer. It is a giant step in the separation of our lives from real experience. As André Collard has written in *Trivia* #2:

Disconnecting Mother Earth from what she brings forth is a tradition deeply entrenched in the Western mind. It is most noticeable among the scientific brotherhood, where the reductionistic, mechanistic approach to nature conceals the inability to respond to life with aesthetic emotion. When applied to language, this approach yields a mathematical science based on the mechanics of transmitting information for manipulative purposes rather than on the very real art of communicating experience. Not surprisingly, computer 'language' derives from such studies.

It is important to remember, as we use our electric lights, drive our cars, or consider word processors that it is not merely the motives of those employing technology which are at issue. We believe feminist goals must be to reconnect with living creatures and the earth, to try to lead self-sustaining lives with some understanding of the lives of other humans, creatures, and of the earth. We must question just what is appropriate technology, while we recognize the damage computer thinking is doing and will increasingly do to our lives. Chrystos, a Native American woman, writing about our participation in technology in *This Bridge Called My Back* asks: "Who is not guilty of being a thief? Who among us gives back as much as we take? Who among us has enough respect? Does anyone know the proper proportions?" ✱

Part-time worker Stephanie Zinowski in the Bloodroot kitchen.

Ethical Vegetarianism

IT IS IMPORTANT TO EXPLAIN once again why we, as feminists, are ethical vegetarians.[1] It is amazing to us that so many human animals don't want to know that other thinking and feeling creatures (the overwhelming majority of them female[2]) are tortured and killed so that we may eat meat or consume "safely" tested drugs and cosmetics. As Carol Adams writes: "Feminists explain sexism through animal metaphors, while unquestioningly accepting the speciesism which permits animal abuse. The implication is that how we treat other animals is lamentable if they were anything but non-human animals. We should remember that while women may *feel* like a piece of meat, and *be treated* like pieces of meat, animals are pieces of meat."[3]

Adams conceptualizes human stages of eating as fourfold: the first is characterized by reliance on plant foods in societies where the first tools enabled women to collect plant proteins to bring back to children and community. The second stage was predominantly vegetarian with some reliance on hunting, typified by Native Ameri-

---

1. Other connections between animal oppression and sexism have been explored brilliantly by **Aviva Cantor** in "The Club, the Yoke, & the Leash," ***Ms. Magazine***, August 1983: "Nowhere is patriarchy's iron fist as naked as in the oppression of animals, which serves as the model and training ground for all other forms of oppression. Its three basic strategies—the club, the yoke, and the leash—operate similarly in the oppression of women and minorities. The club strategy is to kill animals for gain, sadistic pleasure, and the 'affirmation of manhood.' It is domination through brute force. The yoke strategy is to domesticate animals to carry burdens and pull vehicles; supply eggs, wool, and milk; and provide flesh and skins. It is domination through enslavement. The leash strategy is to tame animals to provide the psychic benefits of direct rule of master over pet. It is domination through deceit."

2. If we consider the number of individual animals eaten, they are overwhelmingly female (poultry). On a pound for pound basis, males (as beef) are probably eaten in comparable amounts. From conversations with **Carol Adams** & **Jim Mason**.

3. **Carol Adams**, *The Edible Complex*, awaiting publication.

cans. Third stage eating used domesticated animals together with plant proteins and centered on dairy production. (The racism of imposing dairy dependency on various peoples of color who can't tolerate milk products as happened in North America should be obvious. Continents such as Africa and North America before both were taken over by Europeans used no dairy products, and lactose intolerance is more widespread than is realized. Humans are the only mammals to use milk after infancy.) Finally, it is only since World War II that we have entered fourth stage eating—with animals institutionalized in factory farms. (For those who need information on the nature and growth of this "farming" see *Animal Factories* by Jim Mason and Peter Singer.) Besides the reality of this unspeakable cruelty to non-human animals, it is important to recognize that fourth stage eating cannot support itself. The quantity of "animalized"[4] protein assumed necessary for most typical USA diets oppresses and exploits the rest of the world. Note that 7% of the world's population (USA) consumes 30% of the world's animalized protein. Since it takes 17 to 20 pounds of grain or soy beans to produce one pound of edible beef, we are greedy consumers indeed.

Feminist vegetarians, reading mythographers like Joseph Campbell, can see that meat-eating cultures idealize ferocity, the territorial imperative, vitality and virility—what Carol Adams calls "The Blood Culture." Plant-based societies, on the other hand, celebrate a model of the wonder of life—in its cycle of growth and decay, blossom and seed, wherein death and life appear as transformations of a single superordinated, indestructible force. In other words, harvest rather than violence, harmony with slow change of seasons rather than territoriality.

Myths & beliefs of the '80s are extremely health oriented. Almost every magazine cover promotes the current model of muscular anorexia. In the past eight years, Bloodroot customer concern has passed

4. **Carol Adams** uses this word to clarify the fact that plants provide us with all we need in the way of protein. When we eat meat, the vegetables we need for survival have been "animalized."

from issues such as why isn't all our flour whole wheat to why don't we have wheatless bread. *The Political Palate* was criticized for our use of cream and eggs, not because this use exploits animals, but because it is considered unhealthy to eat such fattening foods. At first sugar was evil, now all sweetening is. A few years ago, an extraordinary number of customers worried about mucous-producing foods and suffered from hypoglycemia. Most recently, wheat, corn, and fermentation allergies are surprisingly widespread. The newest "diseases" are eating disorders and ads offering help for these almost overshadow recent ones for stress management. Focus on stress itself by an affluent and privileged community is shocking. Stress has been said to "cause" or (in conjunction with drugs, pollution, junk food, sedentary lifestyle, etc.) is "related to" cancer and other mysterious diseases. As a result health-oriented Americans have become obsessed with meditation, jogging, and stringent diets. No one seems to ask about stress suffered by poverty and starvation, by rape, by torture and murder, by the death of one's children, by twelve hours a day working on computer chips. "Stress Management" is a luxury of the privileged.

We remember when troubles were taken to priests, ministers and rabbis. Then troubles were taken to doctors and psychotherapists. These days nutritionists are thought to have the answers. To gain perspective on the latest fads in health, re-read *For Her Own Good*, (Ehrenreich & English), the appropriate chapter on therapy in Mary Daly's *Gyn/Ecology*, (especially pages 282–285), and Jan Raymond's reflections in *The Transsexual Empire*. While we want to be generous hearted toward those with particular allergies, we are suspicious when there is an air of moral righteousness connected to the new diets. For ourselves, we assume that foods people have eaten for many centuries are likely to continue to be nutritious and that foods lower down on the food chain are less likely to contain concentrations of pollutants.[5] The history of the use of grains, fermented foods and oils is very ancient. What is new is our exceptional dependence on animalized proteins and fats.

Our vegetarianism stems from a broader base of reasoning than that of personal health. It comes from a foundation of thought based on feminist ethics: a consciousness of our connections with other species and with the survival of the earth. Of course we know that a diet based on grains and legumes, vegetables and fruits is personally healthy. But regardless of how much is learned about food combining, vitamins, basic food group needs, or about problems with pollution or chemical additives to meat, the fact remains that dependence on a meat and poultry diet is cruel and destructive to creatures more like ourselves than we are willing to admit—whether we mean turkeys and cows or the humans starved by land wasted for animal farming purposes to feed the privileged few. This is underscored by Martha M., in a letter to *Lesbian Contradiction*, Issue #6, Spring 1984:

5. While we recognize that agribusiness has poisoned the earth and polluted the waters, because meat represents a concentration of these same pollutants, we're still "better off" eating grains and legumes. Political action directed toward fighting agribusiness would be healthier than grain restricted diets.

Even meat-eaters who believe any atrocity is justified if the victim is non-human and the beneficiary is human may want to consider the effects their dietary choices have on other humans and on themselves. We are all dependent, after all, on the rain forests of Central and South America ("the lungs of the world") for the maintenance of the world's ecological balance. And, as Catherine Caufield tells us, "since 1960 more than three quarters of all Central American forests have been destroyed to produce beef, most of which (more than 90%) is exported to the United States." Moreover, "the people who suffer most directly from the conversion of forest to pasture are the Indians who have lived in the forest for hundreds of years." And, "within a very few years of making the (Indians') land uninhabitable and forcing them to move elsewhere, the ranchers themselves will be forced to move on because their cattle will have exhausted the land."

The same thing is happening in the Philippines. As Joan Gussow has written, "It must be emphasized here that we are no longer discussing a justice issue. We have gone beyond the question of whether it is fair for (the food I choose to eat) to be produced at the expense of some poor farmer's survival. It is my survival that is at stake. For what we are discussing here is the continued functioning on a world-wide scale of the system that provides the world with its food. Short of atomic war . . . there is probably no more serious problem that confronts us than the destruction produced by our business-as-usual assaults on the biosystem which sustains us all."

The point is, the devastating effects factory farming has on this earth are not mere coincidence, not simply by-products of a basically OK system. The devastation is a direct and inevitable result of our own attitudes and our own choices. As long as we treat the earth and its creatures as non-spiritual "resources" which exist only—or even primarily—for our benefit, we will continue to tear the world down around us.[6]

6. Commenting on the spiritual quality of meat eating, **Martha M.** writes further: "It is deeply frustrating to me that so few people recognize the connection between the devastating effects of factory farming and the Euro-US culture's de-spiritualization of non-human animals. We accept factory farming, most of us without even thinking about it, because we don't feel any reverence for the lives of non-human animals. A whale or a seal may inspire our imagination or our sentiment. But a cow? Don't be ridiculous! The intensive exploitation of cows—and pigs, sheep, chickens, etc.—is perfectly OK, even though it involves treatment we would never ever allow to be inflicted on an animal we knew or 'identified with.' If it's a cow, we just don't want to know, don't want to even hear about it, because it's just so easy and convenient and

Unless we can learn that the value system inherent in our meat-eating patterns is one of brutality to human, food animals, and wild animals whose habitats are being destroyed, nothing we do for personal health reasons is truly healthy in the end. "For once stripped of their fundamental underpinnings, health issues may become reduced to narcissistic obsessions." (Carol Adams, Chapter 5: "Thinking with our Hearts").

Meanwhile there is a new category of diseases called eating disorders. While psychotherapists and nutritionists claim to treat them, as feminists we require a political and sociological analysis of their proliferation. First it is important to recognize that the mania with weight reduction and anorexia/bulimia are different points on the same continuum of hatred for women's bodies. Mary Daly writes, under the heading "The Shrinking of Female Being," in *Gyn/Ecology*:

> So also is a woman preoccupied who obsessively examines herself in a mirror, seeing herself as a parcel of protuberances. She is looking through male lenses. Filled with inspired fixations, she checks to see if hair, eyebrows, lashes, lips, skin, breasts, buttocks, stomach, hips, legs, feet are "satisfactory" . . .

> Gynecological/therapeutic/cosmetic preoccupation conceals the patient's emptiness from her Self. It drives the splintered self further into the state of fixation upon the parts that have become symbols of her lost and prepossessed Self. Reduced to the state of an empty vessel/vassal, the victim focuses desperately upon physical symptoms, therapeutically misinterpreted memories, and "appearance," frantically consuming

Feminist scholar Mary Daly at Bloodroot.

medication, counsel, cosmetics, and clothing to cloak and fill her expanding emptiness. As she is transformed into an insatiable consumer, her transcendence is consumed and she consumes herself.[7]

The multiplicity of diet programs, groups, and books, as well as the frightening increase of anorexia among young women is proof that women have internalized body self-hate.

As Kim Chernin points out in *The Obsession: Reflections on the Tyranny of Slenderness*, appropriate weight is a matter of the decade in which you live. She believes feminism has been accompanied, first in the twenties and then in the seventies, with a backlash of hatred for women of size; Marilyn Monroe would be today's fat woman. "The reason, I say, that 98 percent of women gain back the weight they have lost (in diet programs) is simple—the weight belongs to us by nature."[8] It would seem to follow that if we accept variation in height, skin color, ableism, we should be able to recognize fatness as one of many forms of femaleness. *Shadow On A Tightrope*, a superb collection of writings by fat women, demonstrates that we do not. Edited by Lisa Schoenfielder and Barb Weiser, this book is must reading for those who wish to pursue the connections between anorexia, dieting, and the oppression of fat women, and therefore to appreciate why we need fat politics to understand eating disorders. "Consider that control over our bodies is the bottom line of the women's movement," (by Marjory Nelson, "Fat and Old, Old and Fat"). And "Dieting is starvation, it is self-abuse, it is self-hate" (by Kelly, "Medical Crimes"). Other articles in this book which explore political aspects of negative attitudes on weight include "The Goddess is Fat," "Conversation With Nancy," "Some Thoughts On Fat," and the excellent forward.

The more we explore old cookbooks, recipes from other cultures, or ruminate on what folks ate 50 or

---

comfortable to enjoy the by-products of methodical torture and slaughter." References: **Catherine Caufield** quoted from "Big Mac Devours the Amazon," *Food Monitor*, Sept./Oct. 1982; and **Joan Gussow** quoted from "Food: Wanting & Needing & Providing," *Food Monitor*, July/Aug. 1983.

7. **Mary Daly**, *Gyn/Ecology*, pp. 232–233.

8. **Kim Chernin**, *The Obsession*, p. 30

100 years ago the more apparent it becomes that grains have been the food base of most peoples: rice, wheat, corn, millet, rye, barley, etc. Grains were the staple harvested from the wild or from planted crops. Earliest women gathered grains and devised ways to carry them back for sharing or storing. Fruits and vegetables supplemented the grains. Fish were and are eaten by peoples near water and meat has been used as an occasional condiment. It is only in the post war years that meat has become an obsession in this country: a three-meal-a-day obsession that we are exporting as a value system to other countries, spreading starvation as a result. Grains have been associated with the earth's abundance or what patronizing writers call fertility goddesses.[9] Grains are our mothers. Demeter and wheat and the corn mother are but two examples. Our sustenance and life blood comes from grains. All over the earth, oldest images of both mother and food are personified in Goddesses of grains: Chicomecoatl, the Aztec Goddess of food symbolized by a double ear of corn; Ceres/Demeter, whose recurrent image is wheat or barley; Dewi Sri, the Javanese rice Goddess.[10] Ever since the precepts of psychotherapy have acquired general influence, women have been told our problems are because of our mothers. In the fifties, we were told we were neurotic because of them. Now the latest wrinkle is allergies to wheat, corn, and fermentation, continuing the tradition. We prefer to remember the value of grains, legumes ("that which is gathered"), fruits, whether fresh or fermented, yeasted, brewed, in all stages from seed to decay. These are what sustain us. ✹

9. "MAIZE, MAIS, from the original Haitian: SUSTAINER OF LIFE. She is Blessed Daughter, Seed of Seeds, Sacred Mother among the indigenous peoples of the Western Hemisphere, and known by English-speaking North Americans, simply, as corn. Maize and life are one. The origin histories of Mayan descendants remind all people that our bodies were sculpted by the deities from the dough of ground maize. Growing of the crop and every mouthful of the grain continues the creation of the divine ones. Among the deities, the rites and cultivation of maize, womyn were essential. Among some North American nations, a womon would remove her clothes, alone, in the dark of the moon, to drag them around the newly planted field—a ritual to ensure safety and a plentiful harvest. A womon from the Iroquois, a nation in which womyn had much tribal power, stated, "You should understand that it is the women, not the men who have the function of producing life. If they do the planting, the cornstalk produces two or three ears, and it is that way with everything else they plant." Beverly Brown, "Mais: Sustainer of Life," *Maize*, Vol. 1 No. 1, 1983. Available from Word Weavers, Box 8742, Minneapolis, MN 55408.

10. She is Mother Phosop in Thailand, who is said to be pregnant when the grain is ripening. *Pacific and Southeast Asian Cooking* by **Rafael Steinberg**, *Time Life Books*, pp. 154–155.

Part-time workers Jolie Kitenge & Lailla Osman.

On Collectivity & Work

BLOODROOT IS A COLLECTIVE. We have become stronger in our eight years of working in a women's space. Three of us have been here since the beginning. Losing one of our collective members this past year tested our strengths and made us consider carefully how we feel about work and our way of living, as well as how this intersects with feminism and our politics. We are told our longevity is unusual, and this seems to be so. Because losing someone we worked with for six years, someone whose vision had seemed so similar to our own is painful, it is important for us to consider what makes our way of life a continuing satisfaction for the three of us, while we understand that this may not be true for others.

Perhaps one reason it works for us is that the way we work and live is more whole than is generally possible; it is of a piece, organic. We live our work and work our lives. Our rewards are daily because we live what we believe. However, there is much that is very demanding about our work. It requires long hours in our place of business. While it is varied, it is also often pressured. Fortunately we like each other's company as well as the company of women who work with us part time. We continue to be fed by the ideas of other women.[1] As we work, we spend much of our time talking about books and the ideas in them. We're still glad for the garden in the summer, as well as the rest from it in the winter. A heavy snowfall means serenity, knitting, refinishing furniture, or simply sitting and talking.

There is very little room in our lives for anything else but Bloodroot. Some of us reflect on the convent (or Beguine[2]) lives of women where each hour of the day was predetermined. It is a satisfaction to us to have removed from our lives much of what Mary Daly calls the presence of absence: for example, television, and much of the other "entertainment" patriarchy provides. Often we must forgo feminist events. On rare occasions, when one of us dearly wants to hear a speaker or go to a women's concert, we can usually arrange it. We all wanted to go to the Women In Print Conference in Washington, D.C. in 1981, and took our vacation accordingly.

The longer we work in a space informed by women's values, the clearer becomes the discrepancy between our lives and the culture at large. As a result, our judgments seem more clearcut to us. The more one withdraws from patriarchy and its ideas, the easier it is to see the destructiveness and fragmentation inherent in it. It is understandable that many women are suspicious of judgment-making since so many of patriarchy's judgments are used against women's best interests. It is hard to hold different values from those generally assumed by society. However, has Mary Daly has written in *Pure Lust*:

Women who settle for a partial break from patriarchy while failing to sustain and further the feminist vision—for example, by combining non-traditional life styles with male-identified activism or tokenized professionalism—may be "liberated" from the onus of the incarnate male presence just sufficiently to lose touch with the real horrors of patriarchy.

Thus even the conditions of physical separation/freedom, which are so important for the development of a radical feminist analysis, are—in the absence of rigorous Elemental thinking —converted into servitude to the patriarchal system.[3]

---

[1]. In 1983 we doubled our bookstore space to accommodate old and new volumes that continue to nourish our spirits. Just as in *The Political Palate*, we hope to whet your appetite for our favorite books by quoting from them, and you will find them listed in the bibliography at the end of this book.

[2]. "The Beguines" by **Gracia Clark** describes the collective and highly autonomous political, economic and social systems developed in cities by women from the twelfth through fourteenth centuries in Europe. *Quest*, Vol. 1, #4.

[3]. Mary Daly, *Pure Lust*, p. 143.

Women who perceive themselves as different or as defiant are also demanding tolerance or support for pornography, or what they see as a feminist "right" to sadomasochism, not understanding that these reflect phallocracy's growing contempt for women. As women hesitate to make judgments lest we be judged, we should consider Cheri Lesh's words:

It is time to stop pointing fingers and making scapegoats. Time to look at something very hard and real. We are all crazy and weird about sex. Heirs to thousands of years of degradation and torture, of man as S and woman as M, of white as S and non-white as M, of God as S and human as M, of civilization as S and nature as M—who among us can claim immunity, who among us has not tasted the whip sting of poison in the honey, has not confused the slap with the caress? Sadomasochism is the basic sexual perversion of Patriarchy.[4]

Tolerance for the rights of pornographers or for SM practices derive from general support for the values of new and old religions and their current incarnation as psychotherapies, whether the pop types such as EST or the latest in gestalt and neo-Jungian, without recognition that these are used by patriarchy to contain women's legitimate rage and to destroy our memories and hopes. See work by Florence Rush, Phyllis Chesler, Jeffrey Masson, as well as Mary Daly:

4. **Cheri Lesh**, "Hunger & Thirst in the House of Distorted Mirrors," *Against Sadomasochism*, pp. 202–203.

Just as Naming passions involves identifying the agent and object . . . so also an adequate Naming of feminism requires Naming the stoppers as well as the direction of this movement. All else is therapy, psychobabble, therapy, self-hatred, therapy, futility.[5]

Presumably many wish to live and work in an integrated fashion without oppressing others—a hard dream to attain—and very different from the ways we have been taught to live or what we are taught are appropriate and expected pleasures. We have all learned to separate our lives into divisions/fragments: work during week in order to be able to play during weekends; work to earn leisure time; work to earn money to buy things that are supposed to make us happy. Living for real in the present means giving up the plastic world we're used to. Most women have little choice or means to escape the fragmentation

5. Daly, op. cit., p. 206, Florence Rush, *The Best Kept Secret*; Phyllis Chesler, *Women & Madness*; Jeffrey Masson, *The Assault on Truth*.

Poet & feminist theorist Audre Lorde.

that patriarchy considers the norm. As a result, a token few women are rewarded with high salaries for meaningless work, some of it occasionally interesting, while the assumption is that *everyone's* life takes place after business hours, on weekends or vacations. We are trying to live differently. As Audre Lorde has written:

The lack of concern for the erotic root and satisfactions of our work is felt in our disaffection from so much of what we do. For instance, how often do we truly love our work?

The principal horror of any system which defines the good in terms of profit rather than in terms of human need, or which defines human need to the exclusion of the psychic and emotional components of that need—the principal horror of such a system is that it robs our work of its erotic value, its erotic power and life appeal and fulfillment. Such a system reduces work to a travesty of necessities, a duty by which we earn bread or oblivion for ourselves and those we love. But this is tantamount to blinding a painter and then telling her to improve her work, and to enjoy the act of painting. It is not only next to impossible, it is also profoundly cruel.

As women, we need to examine the ways in which our world can be truly different. I am speaking here of the necessity for reassessing the very quality of all the aspects of our lives and of our work.[6]

There is much about Bloodroot that is wonderful and beautiful. Yet the maintenance of it requires commitment, devotion and lots of hard work (as does any very small business, but particularly the restaurant business). But we do go further, because we love our reading and we talk while we cook. Both our way of life and our reading make us intensely aware of extremity: the extremity of women's lives, the earth's life. It means our beliefs, our actions, our behavior, are all part of this intensity, this consciousness of extremity. We choose this consciousness. We choose living fully as we work. We choose work we believe in. For us, this kind of work, living, and time spent is breath and blood. ✲

6. **Audre Lorde**, "Uses of the Erotic: The Erotic as Power," *Out & Out Pamphlet* #3.

On Collectivity & Work

Pat Shea, Selma, Denslow Brown, Noel, Betsey Beaven, Barbara Beckelman, Samn Stockwell, and unidentified woman celebrating Bloodroot's one-year anniversary, 1978.

In Selma's garden at home.

A Witch Recipe for Grievers

SOMETIMES NOTHING CAN BE DONE to change things, and hurt and anger must be transmuted: examples include the death of someone loved, permanent body damage like breast cancer, dissolution of relationship. See what you can use from this "recipe."

1. In the middle of the worst pain, try to find something to make, to create for yourself.
Something difficult and particularly rewarding. Even if you can't start it now, plan to start it soon. Something that will last. Write something, sew something. Use your own special, already polished skill to plan and create a lasting present for yourself. Women used to make mourning quilts and embroideries.[1]

1. See **Judy Chicago's** *Embroidering Our Heritage*.

2. Consider your friends.
Withdraw from ones who are frightened by your pain, the ones who think there might have been something you could have done, should still do to change things, the ones who want to be "fair." Remember you have a right to judge and to be angry. Don't forget Hecate. When you're hurting, you need

especially considerate tenderness. As lonely as you may feel, it's better to have fewer or no friends than those who won't care to understand. Perhaps it is fear of friends' lack of sensitivity which sends so many women to therapists—to pay for a supposedly nonjudgmental caring with a hidden agenda of "fitting" into the therapist's norms, whatever those may be.

3. Take charge of your sorrow.
It will take some time to project ahead and think when the pain will be over, but with effort, you'll be able to see that end. Pain comes in and out like waves. When it recedes, you may feel it is over. Then another wave engulfs you. That's when you remember that there will be a time when it will be past—a time you can name. Not next week, not next month. Maybe in three months. Maybe not until Fall, or Spring. Whenever it is, set it as a goal. Know you can survive until then. Meanwhile, take the time between to make an ending ritual. Jews burn a candle for 5 days after a loved one dies. The candle is in a tall glass, and as the flame burns lower the upper part of the glass darkens until the flame goes out by itself and the glass is all dark. Other candles are lit on the anniversary of the death, and on particular holidays.

Create a ritual. Remember—a ritual has symbolic meaning—so whatever you choose to do must have significance for you. And a ritual must be repetitive. You must be able to do it again and again—times when you don't seem to need it, and times when you can't imagine that it will help. For example—a candle can be marked off in days and burned, a little each day. Maybe pictures or letters should be burned or, if you prefer, torn in small pieces and sent off in running water—a little each day or week, until the bad time is past. Sometimes anger requires a hex. Remember, Z Budapest has said a witch that cannot hex cannot heal.

4. Remember the healing power of work, if it is work you love and in which you believe.

Remember a feminist is a woman who recognizes the common oppression of women and will struggle against it. We need to imagine repairing, reweaving, mending the damage done, as Mary Daly points out, and then to do it.

How to be a Griever's Friend

A griever's friend is one who is there, who spends more time than seems reasonable with a griever. She listens and understands. She isn't Pollyanna. She's angry at her friend's pain. She values loyalty over fairness. She doesn't say *"you should have"* or *"why didn't you"* or *"now you should,"* and she tries not to let the griever think that way about herself. She tells the griever over and over that what has happened is not fair, not deserved; that anger is justified.

A Note On Dying

Maybe it is not until our own death becomes imminent, palpable, that we can consider how we live. Those of us who have been told we have some fatal disease are faced with choices about our living, now. Of course, we all know someday we will die, yet we don't know it until we are told the day is near, is set. Then the remainder of living is thrown into sharp focus, whether it is daily behavior or what we let the doctors do to delay the event. Certainly the 1 in 4 women with breast cancer must face this reality. Those of us who have spent time with someone dying, when it is not taken entirely from our hands by the medical profession, and when it is not sudden and/or violent, know that it is a transformation that possesses its own wonder, triumph, and joy. ✲

See **Audre Lorde**'s poems & *Cancer Journals*, **Elizabeth Dodson Gray**'s *Patriarchy as a Conceptual Trap*, & the writings of Starhawk.

Part-time Bloodroot

1977–

From the earliest days of Bloodroot, many women who are not full-time members of the collective have performed important roles. Many are featured in photographs throughout this book; here are more.

Charlene LaVoie, a part-time worker since 1977, volunteers her legal services in addition to working in the kitchen once a month.

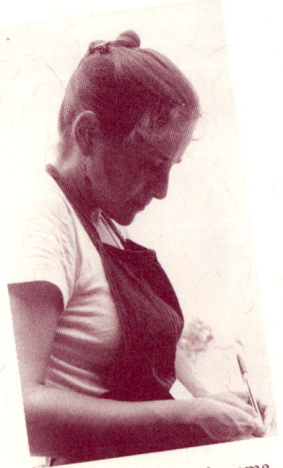

Barbara Beckelman became a part of Bloodroot when it was a feminist cooperative in Selma's home.

Krystyna Colburn has provided payroll & bookkeeping services since the early days of Bloodroot.

Carolanne Curry has been a close friend & advisor of Bloodroot since 1988.

Cats have always been popular at Bloodroot. This is **Aphrodite**.

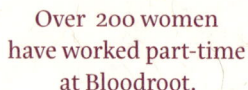

Over 200 women have worked part-time at Bloodroot.

Teri Keiser

Marie Gall

Alison Dunn & Rose Lauture

Part-Time Bloodroot

Maggie Dunford

Sandy Anderson & Donna Osborne

Connie Busch

Rachel Portnoy

Vegan cook **Lagusta Yearwood** collaborated on the *Best of Bloodroot Volumes I & II*.

Some faces of Bloodroot in the 21st century.

Jessika Rene

Erica Garcia & Tara Rubano

Part-Time Bloodroot

Carol Graham

Angelique Vanterpool

Suzanne Beck & Valerie Wilke

Noel & Selma.

The Perennial Political Palate

1993

The Perennial Political Palate is the third cookbook published by the Bloodroot Collective as Sanguinaria Publishing. The introduction to the book—the essay that follows—remains one of Selma's favorite essays 27 years later.

In a post to her blog (selmaslist.blogspot.com, April 5, 2012), *Selma again reflects upon persistence:*

"In 1977, several friends and I started Bloodroot. Why? Because my change from housewife and mother to lesbian feminist meant that I needed to lead a life outside patriarchal morality away from husband and societal expectations. I wanted a community with shared values (not all, but most), and I wanted to think and put into practice what was feminism for me. This has been my 35-year work in progress shared by Noel Furie, and others who have been with us at Bloodroot.

So my "coming out" was not about a sexual choice, though it included that; it was not about getting married to a woman instead of a man and going on to lead a couple's life similar to that of heterosexuals.

It meant trying to lead a life that was better. Better for people and creatures and the earth itself as well as for myself. We hoped for community. And while of course there have been changes, mostly this choice, these choices have made that possible.

But how could we, Noel and I, keep doing this for 35 years? We can because it is so deeply satisfying to us. We like the people who come to be fed by us, very much. We still like cooking very much. We can't imagine a different life ... We love the idea of eating what is in our gardens or at the farmers' market this minute, totally glutting on strawberries in June and apples in September.

But we are also thrilled to explore traditional people's comfort foods, and so will search out imported Haitian or Jamaican or Mexican or Greek or Korean ingredients to make the dishes of which our workers and friends have shared recipes. The result is that we can look forward to each season's menus with many more options than those whose plates center on meat.

Our customers don't have to be vegetarians, and many are not. But where can they get homemade bread like ours, or soups as satisfying? We want to seduce them with delicious vegan food, and to encourage them to eat less or no meat."

On Persistence & Feminism

A PERENNIAL IS A PLANT which dies down to the ground each winter and then returns to life in the spring, the roots being the maintaining force of life.[1] In contrast an annual is one which flowers, sets seed in a season and dies. The word perennial, from *per-annum* means through the years. Bloodroot the plant is a perennial. Bloodroot, the feminist restaurant and bookstore has survived sixteen winters, sustaining her owners' feminist vision as well as keeping minds and bodies fed.

There is much talk these days in academic circles of the first and second waves of feminism, as well as the possibility that we are now entering a third. In these circles, the implications are that the struggle for women's suffrage was a distinct beginning, starting in the latter part of the nineteenth century and completed in the early part of the twentieth; and that a second consciousness arose in the late sixties until the mid-eighties. Of course, a careful perusal of women's writings that managed to make it into print and survive shows that feminism has existed through the years.[2] Feminism is a perennial. Regardless of which wave patriarchal time assumes us to be in, feminist roots have always existed, as

1. There are herbaceous perennials and shrubby perennials. The latter maintain twigs, stems and branches when leaves have dropped. There are also evergreen perennials.

2. e.g. **Virginia Woolf**, especially in *Three Guineas* (New York: Harcourt, Brace, Jovanovich, 1938), **Ruth Herschberger** in *Adam's Rib* (New York: Pellegrini and Cudahy, 1948), and **Simone de Beauvoir** in *The Second Sex* (New York: Alfred A. Knopf, Inc., 1952), all writing between the so-called "waves."

evidenced by women in resistance. There have always been women who wouldn't accept what men wanted of them, always women who fought rapists, and always women who didn't want to be pregnant. There have always been women who imagined and created life without violence, war, and murder, and always women who have been healers. It's not that *all* women have been so, but there have always been *some*. There are times that seem like winter to feminists, and there are always women who tell the men what they want to hear,[3] but others resist and wait through the winter for a warming sun and spring rain. Some may die, the land being too poor, but others find fertile ground and persist.

While there is beauty to be found in annuals, gardeners do need perennials. Because we believe in return and survival, we decided to call this book *The Perennial Political Palate*. Our earlier books are *The Political Palate* and *The Second Seasonal Political Palate*.

OUR HISTORY. In 1977 there were a number of women who felt the influence of feminism strongly enough to put their beliefs into effect, using the resources available to them, by starting feminist businesses. We were among them. It was impossible for those of us who started Bloodroot to proceed with our lives in the same way once our consciousness changed. We had to change our circumstances and hope to change those of other women as well.

For us this endeavor took the form of a restaurant and a bookstore, both "feminist." The bookstore was easy to stock; there were a growing number of feminist presses producing books of interest.[4] The restaurant would have to be vegetarian. Only by refusing to use the flesh of other creatures and therefore economizing on the earth's riches so that more might eat could we call our food feminist. It seemed appropriate to call our venture Bloodroot (the common name of a North American wild-

3. Such as Clarence Thomas' women friends at the Congressional hearings of his Supreme Court nominations. Since they haven't been sexually harassed, they couldn't believe Anita Hill could have been.

4. Feminist publishing companies active in the '70s included: Daughters Inc., Persephone Press, Diana Press, The Feminist Press, Naiad Press, Moon Books, Booklegger, The Women's Press (of England), The Women's Press (of Canada), Frog in the Well, Women's Press Collective, Speculum Press, Violet Press, Spinsters Ink, Pearlchild, Cassandra Publications, Elf and Dragon Press, Kids Can Press, New Seed Press, and Ata Books.

Bloodroot under construction, 1990s—the drop ceiling was removed to expose the dining room's rafters.

BLOODROOT

a feminist restaurant/bookstore
with a seasonal vegetarian menu

ON THE SOUND

in Black Rock (Bridgeport) Ct.
5 minutes from exit 24 on I95
25 minutes from New Haven
1½ hours from New York City
at 85 Ferris St. Bridgeport, Ct.

We are looking for flatware,
old dishes, old pictures of women,
and creditors

Detail from flyer before Bloodroot's opening in March 1977.

flower),[5] though the name upset some people then, and still continues to puzzle a few now. The word *Bloodroot* apparently connotes something disturbing to these people. We don't know why. Our blood is fed by vegetables, those that grow below ground as well as those that grow above. What can possibly be considered bad about blood? Perhaps it evokes an ancient fear of women's blood (menstruation). When customers ask, we show them a page in our first cookbook describing the plant and its manner of growth: the way the rhizomes branch, each piece sending up its own leaf furled vertically around a single flower. It was our intention to form a working collective like that, an interdependence, each separate and individual, independent but joined.

We considered ourselves radical feminist lesbians in 1977, and we still do. We didn't encounter Mary Daly's definition of radical feminism until 1984, when she wrote *Pure Lust*, but we then found it strikingly appropriate to what we were attempting. Her definition has four parts. First, a woman feels "an awesome sense of otherness from patriarchal norms and values." Second, she has a consciousness of the "sadosociety's sanctions against radical feminism." Third, she feels "rage at the oppression of all sisters of all races, ethnic groups, and nations—an identification with woman as woman." And finally, a radical feminist persists despite the odds, when others decide that feminism is a phase that has passed, or that is out of "fashion."[6]

The question was (and still is), how does one take these words and put them into concrete action? We needed to do that. The word that best described our state of mind in 1977 was desperate. We *had* to make a change, for our souls' sake. We were determined—even though we had no business skills to speak of. It took a leap of faith (and some money) to do something we felt we had to do. It was our sense of otherness that required us to set aside caution and do something radical with our lives.

5. The drawing of the bloodroot flower that we use as our logo is the work of botanic artist **Laura Louise** ("Timmy") **Foster**. She and her husband **Lincoln Foster** tended what was arguably the most beautiful wildflower garden in the world on Canaan Mountain in Northwest Connecticut. Both now deceased, their love of the earth and its plants, as well as their intelligence and generosity remain a gift to us.

6. Daly, Mary, *Pure Lust: Elemental Feminist Philosophy*, Boston: Beacon Press, 1984, pp. 396–397.

Those who took primary responsibility for Bloodroot have changed through the years, though there are three who have persisted. Many have come to work part-time, and left, and some work part-time and have stayed. Sometimes the leavings have been painful. When we work hard with each other, laugh at the same jokes, argue, and learn from each other's lives, of course we love those with whom we have grown in struggle. Sometimes the separations are sad, but not painful. That's how it is in the garden, in the restaurant, and in our lives. We can't imagine otherwise.

PLACE. We cherish a small piece of land on an inlet of Long Island Sound in Bridgeport, Connecticut. Bridgeport is an extreme example of an industrial city suffering seriously from the callous and selfish economic practices of the eighties, as well as earlier times. The city is largely African-American, Latina, and Asian. Its riches are in its cultural diversity, its strong, outspoken people. We are proud to be a part of it. Yet a few years ago, an entrepreneur across the harbor decided that the city should take our land by eminent domain so that he could expand his amusement-park ideas of what is good for Bridgeport. Luckily, neighbors joined us to defeat the proposal, so our waterfront still remains beach plums and shore roses, which we planted over the broken cement fill dumped there by an earlier owner. (Some say we have persisted like the roses, complete with thorns, which thrive over the broken cement.)

More recently, representatives of the sadosociety attempted to build a regional medical waste plant right next to a city housing project, to further pollute our air. There are also continued attempts to make Bridgeport the garbage incineration center of the Northeast. Many people in Bridgeport, ourselves among them, struggle to keep those perversions under control. Bridgeport's financial problems and past inept leadership have been a problem to all in

The outdoor patio at Bloodroot.

the area. These are issues we can't ignore; we are all affected.

In 1977 we started Bloodroot in Bridgeport in what had once been a machine shop. It took about three years after we opened before people came to us in enough numbers to make a livelihood possible. Many of those who came and continue to come most frequently, make it clear that the sense of otherness that inspired us to start a place like Bloodroot is something they feel too. We are constantly heartened by them. We enjoy an unusually high repeat business. We seem to be an oasis for many.[7] Because we don't wait tables, a customer places her or his order at the desk, gives their name which is written at the top of the slip, then takes the slip to the counter separating the kitchen from the dining room. When the meal is ready, the name is called, and the meal picked up. Customers are asked to clear their own tables. This procedure encourages informality and a feeling of parity which obviously pleases those who return often, and keeps away those who don't care for this kind of atmosphere. Of course, provision is made for those who do need assistance.

PURPOSE. People often remark, when they return after several years absence, that the consistency of quality is surprising. We work hard to achieve this. Persistence is important to us, not only in making our food as delicious as possible, but also in remembering our purpose. We must look at each issue in terms of a feminist overview—how women are affected by whatever happens within Bloodroot, as well as without.

Although we are concerned with both global and local issues of our planet, we are here for women; that is our purpose. It is why the word feminist appears in our logo and over our door. It is why the thirty-foot long wall that faces the view of the Sound is covered with old photographs of women. We have a bulletin board in the foyer with items of

---

7. Many of our customers are men, and some also seem to feel a sense of "otherness." This is in contrast to our early days, when it was a rare man indeed who was interested in radical feminism, though there were many who assumed that feminists would share liberal values. See *Right Wing Women* by **Andrea Dworkin** (New York: Putnum-Perigree, 1983), for a critical analysis of this. These days there are a few books written by men that can be called pro-feminist (such as *Men On Rape* by **Timothy Beneke**, *Refusing to be a Man* by **John Stoltenberg**, *Men Confront Pornography* edited by **Michael Kimmel**, & *Final Analysis* by **Jeffrey Mason**) and better yet, some men are reading them and wanting to actively change themselves as well as other men. We like to believe we reinforce feminist values in men who are different and who are struggling to reject sexism.

political interest to women. We play women's music whenever we are open. A sign above the kitchen opening indicates our disparagement of calorie counting, and in another sign we attempt to discuss control of unruly children without mother-blaming. We are proud that the variety of our foods, the pictures on the wall, as well as our books and the music we play reflects the diversity of women's ethnic and racial backgrounds.

We are also here for the animals. At the beginning none of us were vegetarian, but we were convinced of the importance of vegetarianism by animal rights friends.[8] For the first three years we served fish on summer weekends, but then stopped. Rather quickly our hearts followed what the mind already agreed was rational—that eating meat is wrong for cruelty to creatures who can feel and experience pain, and wrong because it contributes to worldwide starvation, mostly of women and children. More recently we have become increasingly aware that rainforest destruction kills our Mother Earth as well. Serious worldwide environmental decline is the result of the development of global acceptance of factory-style farming and the promotion of the false idea that meat consumption is necessary for a good life.[9] We have become passionate vegetarians as part and parcel of our feminism. As a result, it is upsetting when others don't seem to be able to learn to make the connections that have become obvious to us. Speciesism has similarities to racism and sexism, and obvious differences (for instance, animals can't vote or lobby for themselves).

Yet racism, sexism, and speciesism all share a common denominator.[10] Our priority is not to establish which evil seems primary, but rather to set ourselves against them all in whatever ways we can. To try, anyway.[11]

As a consequence of our evolving consciousness, our menu has become less dairy-oriented. These days we are sure to offer vegan soups, salads, entrées,

8. **Priscilla Feral** & **Jim Mason** initially inspired our decision to be vegetarian. Both are animal rights activists still. **Jim Mason** is one of the exceptional men who has tried to make the connections between oppressions. The author of *Animal Factories* (New York, NY: Crown Publishers, Paperback, 1984) he is well-read in radical feminist literature and is working on a general history/philosophy book on the origins of the patriarchy and of animal domestication (as yet unnamed) to be published by Simon & Shuster. Watch for it.

9. *Worldwatch Paper 103: Taking Stock: Animal Farming and the Environment*, July 1991. (1776 Massachusetts Ave NW, Washington DC, 20036). This $5.00 pamphlet is the most in-depth analysis of factory farming and the resulting global human starvation and ecological destruction that we have seen.

10. "All of us, women and men alike, are conditioned to conform to this culture. Men are trained to be dominators, women to be subordinates. No one is exempt," writes **Kay Leigh Hagan** in her article "Orchids In The Arc-

tic" in *Ms. Magazine*, Vol. 11, No. 3. The common denominator in these various oppressions is a dominator. For further reading, see *The Dreaded Comparison, Human and Animal Slavery* by Marjorie Spiegel (New York: Mirror Books, 1988).

11. It is heartening to have books such as **Carol Adams'** *The Sexual Politics Of Meat, A Feminist-Vegetarian Critical Theory* (New York: Continuum Publishing, 1991), as well as organizations such as **Feminists For Animal Rights** (PO BOX 10017, North Berkeley Sta., Berkeley, CA 94709), and **Ecofeminist Visions Emerging** (40 West 46th Street, NYC, NY 10036). The book and the organizations make the connections that we are trying to make, as has **Josephine Donovan** in *Signs*, Vol. 15, No. 2, "Animal Rights and Feminist Theory." To subscribe to FAR (Feminists for Animal Rights), write to Batya Bauman, PO BOX 694, Cathedral Sta., NYC, NY 10025.

12. The argument for a vegan diet is convincingly made in *For The Vegetarian in You* by **Billy Ray Boyd**, (San Francisco: Taterhill Press, 1987).

and desserts. We want to be sure vegans can eat well and with diversity at Bloodroot. We've altered some recipes and created many new ones. There were 52 vegan recipes in *The Political Palate*, 55 in *The Second Seasonal Political Palate*, and 138 of the recipes in this volume (85%) are dairy and egg-free. We eat and cook with less cheese, eggs, and milk. We haven't given them up altogether, but we do give pride of place to recipes that have.[12]

From the beginning, people have thought of Bloodroot as a health food restaurant. Though this might be hard to debate, it's just not where we put our emphasis. Health food fashions change. Some health food stores sell and/or serve "organic" meat, which appalls us. And there are some health food theories about which we are skeptical. When we first opened, some people would only eat whole wheat bread. Now many ask for wheat-free bread. Some have been told that fermented foods such as soy sauce or beer or anything with yeast should be avoided. Some won't eat any foods with sweeteners in them at all, whether honey, maple syrup, or sugar. Of course we always discuss ingredients with anyone who wants to know the details of our cooking, and we are especially careful about accommodating particular allergies, but we find ourselves suspicious of prohibitions on traditional ingredients that have a long history of healthy use.

Right now fat is considered the greatest danger, not just animal fats, but oils as well. Meanwhile, there is no recognition of the long and healthy lives that Mediterranean peoples have enjoyed for centuries while liberally flavoring their food with olive oil, and there is no regard for that fact that Asian or African countries depend on palm or coconut for nourishment. A recent extensive study of 6,500 Chinese people showed them low in cancer, heart disease, and diabetes until they adopted a higher meat diet as in the West.[13] Yet their use of cooking oil is high. Also, in contrast to most health food "wisdom," we find calorie counting and other anti-fat activities offensive. In some of the anti-fat sentiment we find anti-fat women sentiment. This is oppressive—not only to women of size, but to all of us. Many women are forced to be anorexic or bulimic rather than be fat. Fat is virtually always a cosmetic issue, but people pretend it is a health issue.[14] It's not that we're not interested in good health; we are. But we're more sympathetic to vegan concerns than to health fashions. Of course, we try to use organic produce as much as possible. Most of all we want to use local produce in season for economic and aesthetic reasons. Just compare a strawberry or a tomato grown and ripened locally with one which has traveled across the country.

All of us garden, although there's no way we can produce enough for our restaurant even though our gardens are fairly large. The best use of our earth is for herbs and a few lettuces, squash, and tomatoes. It is necessary to get our hands in the earth each year, to try to figure out what She will grow with us, whether it is the garlic leaves and shiso, the blueberries which take so long to pick, or the daisies and the butterfly weed, the poppies and the nigella ("Love-in-a-mist": the source of czarnuszka seed for our rye bread). This past summer we were blessed with an abundance of kale for soup, an endless supply of Chinese cabbage for salads and stir-fries, generous amounts of Swiss chard, green beans, tomatillos (for Salsa Verde), and elderberries, tomatoes, cucumbers, and pears!

ECONOMICS. It has been hard for women who want to change the unfair economic realities of patriarchy to think practically about how to make a business viable. The long hours of labor needed to make bread, to chop vegetables for soup, to devise our always changing menu, and the endless hours needed to wash dishes, dishes, dishes, don't support for long the form of thinking that says "food should

13. As reported in *The New York Times*, Tuesday May 8, 1991

14. See *The Obsession: Reflections on the Tyranny of Slenderness* by **Kim Chernin** (New York: Harper & Row, 1981), and *Shadow on a Tightrope*, edited by **Lisa Schoenfielder** & **Barb Weiser** (San Francisco, Aunt Lute, 1983), for more information on fat oppression..

be cheap." While our prices are substantially lower than other restaurants in our area, we do have to factor in enough so that we can make a decent living and pay a fair wage. We love the political conversations we have while chopping onions, but we also need time for ourselves, and the wherewithal to support it.

Within the women's community there have been many discussions about class.[15] These are often confusing as we try to understand our differences. We all differ in regard to our backgrounds: our families' access to money, their attitudes and ethical/political values, and their ethnicity or race. As each of us reflect on where we have come from (of course with strong emotion), we attempt to understand and perhaps to force ourselves into a particular class category. Here at Bloodroot we have begun to think it is not possible to fit complex individual experiences into a Marxist structure. For example, where should we slot any of the past or current ethnic peoples who immigrated here, be they Jewish, Italian, Chinese, or Thai, who started or are now opening "family" businesses? Are they capitalists, petit bourgeois, or working class?

Women who grew up poor or who see their childhoods as disadvantaged for one reason or another have spoken of their pain as well as their pride. And women who had more advantages often feel guilty. Those of mixed backgrounds, who find it difficult to fit their experience neatly into a category, may vacillate between guilt and resentment. It is necessary to remember that each of our histories is a mix of painful memories and treasured strengths. We must listen to each other to appreciate our very different points of view and behavior, the hurt as well as the pride.

It is also important to assess how we live today. Women can't be blamed for wanting to live better lives now, and it would seem feminism ought to mean that women should have equal access to the

---

15. See Vol. 4, No. 2, *Lesbian Ethics*, edited by Jeanette Silveira (PO BOX 4723, Albuquerque NM 87196) for a recent & extensive discussion.

Kathy Lewis.

16. Books by **MacKinnon** include *Feminism Unmodified* (Cambridge, MA: Harvard University Press, 1987) and (with **Andrea Dworkin**) *Pornography and Civil Rights* (Durham, NC: Southern Sisters, Inc., 411 Morris Street, 27701, 1988). Books by **Daly** include *Beyond God The Father* (Beacon Press, 1973), *Gyn/Ecology: The Metaethics of Radical Feminism*, 1978, *Pure Lust*, op. cit., *Websters' First New Intergalactic Wickedary of the English Language*, 1987, all Beacon Press, and *Outercourse*, 1992, Harper, San Francisco. Books by **Chesler** include *Women and Madness*, New York: Avon Books, 1972; *Mothers on Trial: The Battle for Children and Custody* (New York: McGraw-Hill, 1986) and The Sacred Bond (New York: Times Books, 1988). Books by **Corea** include *The Hidden Malpractice*, *The Mother Machine*, and *The Invisible Epidemic: The Story of Women and AIDS*, (New York: Harper Collins, 1992).

17. Woolf, op. cit.

18. *The Straight Mind & Other Essays* by Monique Wittig (Boston: Beacon Press, 1992) is a collection of most provocative writings.

same money and power that men have. Obviously, women in the professions can make good use of their abilities to remember women whose choices are limited (see what Catherine MacKinnon makes of law, Mary Daly of academia, Phyllis Chesler of therapy, or Gena Corea of medicine),[16] but becoming a professional can also destroy or undermine a woman's loyalty to her own kind. Virginia Woolf wrote compellingly about this in *Three Guineas*.[17] Women who join the ranks of the professions must be especially cautious about being co-opted by those most responsible for the destruction of our spirits and of all that we value as feminists.

It would seem that there are two possible courses of action for a feminist woman living in the patriarchy. One is to join it, to try to learn its rules, and then subvert it from within, to be what Monique Wittig[18] called (speaking of writing and language) a Trojan Horse. And so women become doctors, lawyers, administrators, or run for Congress, finding careers in fields previously entirely male. Hopefully when we exist in those categories in enough numbers we will make a significant difference. Unfortunately, right now most women trained in patriarchy's ways internalize patriarchal values. It is not impossible to imagine a radical feminist professional, but in practical terms, it is of infrequent occurrence.

There is another route a woman can take. She can decide to remain outside the patriarchy as much as she can, the better to critique it. But then the problem is that there is no format, no formulated "way" to proceed to make one's living and to keep our spirits healthy and whole. In contrast one can decide to become a lawyer or a doctor and learn what routes, though difficult and costly, to take to get to those goals. But to survive and not become a "professional," we have fewer or no choices. One can get a factory job or clean houses or do computer

19. Woman are invisible to ourselves. Note the prevalence of the word "guys" to address a room full of women.
20. See *Worldwatch Paper #110 Gender Bias: Roadblock to Sustainable Development* by **Jodi L. Jacobson** (1776 Massachusetts Ave NW, Washington, DC 20036, 1992), & *The War Against Women* by **Marilyn French** (New York: Summit Books, 1992). Also **Vandana Shiva**, in *Staying Alive: Women, Ecology & Development* (London: Zed Books, 1989) argues that modern scientific knowledge and economic development intentionally destroy the earth and women's livelihood. "People are perceived as poor if they eat millets (grown by women) rather than commercially produced and distributed processed foods sold by global agri-business. They are seen as poor if they live in self-built housing made from natural material like bamboo and mud rather than in cement houses. They are seen as poor if they wear handmade garments of natural fiber rather than synthetics. Subsistence, as culturally perceived poverty, does not necessarily imply a low physical quality of life." (p. 10). She explains the failure of the "green revolution" and why famine is becoming increasingly widespread after traditional ways of staying alive are destroyed by "development" and "progress." The pamphlet and both books are must reading for feminists in that the discussion treats of women's situations in other countries and across class lines.

work, but find little or no satisfaction or gratification in that work.

Outside the context of these non-choices, we must realize that there is another parallel world in which women form community and do work unvalued and uncounted by the patriarchy, and unvalued though considered necessary even to women ourselves.[19] This is true globally, as is discussed by Marilyn French in *The War Against Women*. And so we are unaware of the understructure of all societies and how it is that women maintain while so many men destroy. In modern times liberal forces are undermining whatever hegemony women have had in places such as Africa or India by naming men as heads of households, and by devising cash crop systems thinking this will help alleviate poverty. What it does is give the men more power and money and leaves women, whose responsibility is always the family and community, less resources and less land to plant or from which to forage.[20]

Those invisible women we have been taught to disdain, conventional women of the old traditions, had areas of power, respect, magic—precious and sustaining where they existed. Those of us who live with "progress" have all but lost access to those resources, and modern women have been taught to hold these "old wives' tales" of myth and ritual in contempt. When we imagine where one might find guidance, we can think of ancient women—some of whom set themselves apart from the community, whether as healers or as weird old women. In Western culture we called them witches; native peoples called them shamans. Sometimes there were communities in which women managed, even if briefly,

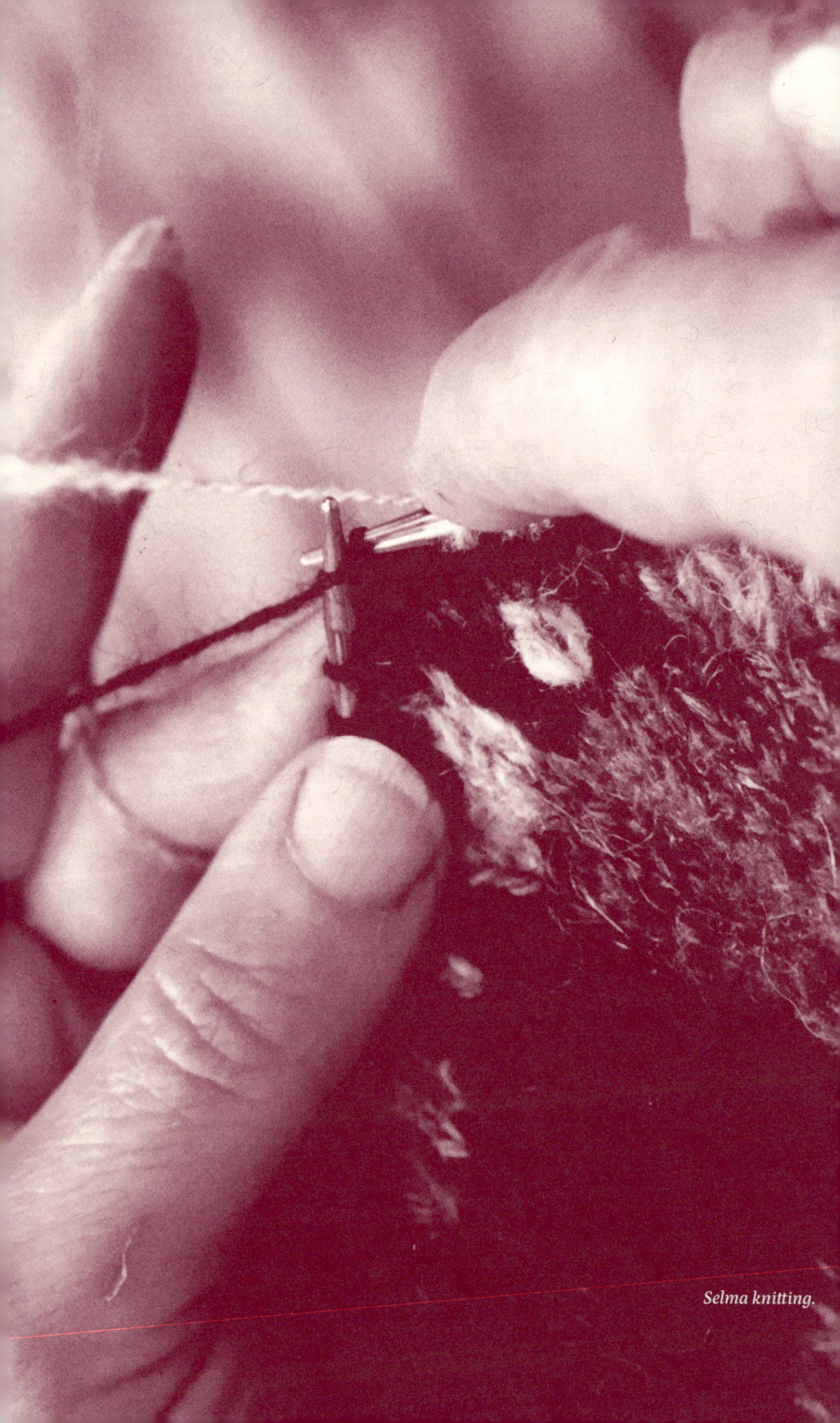

Selma knitting.

to be self-sufficient: such as the Beguines in Europe's Middle Ages or the marriage resisters' communities in pre-communist China (who possessed their own language, inexplicable to men.)[21]

For sustenance, for the sacred in today's world, modern women may be able to find resources in traditional women's work. These forms of labor use very simple technologies which require patience and a lifetime of study. In our industrialized world there are still a few places for a gatherer of wild herbs to go, and there are still basketmakers. Some women learn to be potters, some tend gardens and there has been a return to spinning and weaving. And women have always been knitters.

It's very difficult to explain why these activities, these kinds of work are so gratifying to those who are trying to remember how to do them. Perhaps Paula Gunn Allen's description of the word "mage" (one who does magic) in *Grandmothers of the Light* is the best help to understanding:

The basic nature of the universe of power is magic: the name given to the practice of a mage. Ma ... comes in variants: ma, mo, mu, mi, and me. All are versions of the same morpheme ... and refer one way or another to the Great Mother or Great Goddess of the Indo-Germanic tradition. The Goddess, named variously Ma, Maa, or Maat, was in time demoted and even changed gender over the ages, but she is known even today in her identity as Tiamat, Aphrodite, Ishtar, Astarte, and Isis. She can be discerned in words such as mother, mom, mammary, mutter ... Ma is the essential female syllable ... and at its root designates mystery, mother, and myth, all feminine forces or powers. Ge, another interesting fragment, one from which words such as geology, geomancy, geas, geometry, geophysics, and geopolitical derive, is part of the name of Gea or Gaia ... and refers to those of the Great Goddesses' powers that emanate from her planetary body ... A mage is a shaman or medicine person who specializes in the control and application of the two aspects of the multitudinous Great Goddess(es). Magic refers to the ritual activities of a mage ... ritual actions that result in transformations.[22]

21. See *A Passion for Friends* by **Janice G. Raymond** (Boston: Beacon Press, 1986) and *The New York Times* November 1991, "A Secret Language for Women": "Called everything from 'the witches' script' to the first language of women's liberation, the flowing ideographs were passed from mother to daughter in a secret literary tradition that defied China's male-dominated establishment. The script, known as 'bushy' or 'women's calligraphy' has all but disappeared, surviving only among a dwindling handful of elderly women in one county of a mountainous Hunan province. Nushu, made up of 2,000 individual characters, has been used by women in Hunan for at least 1,000 years."

22. *Grandmothers of the Light: A Medicine Woman's Sourcebook* by **Paula Gunn Allen** (Boston: Beacon Press, 1991), pp. 15–16.

23. **Max Allen**, fabric historian, assembled an exhibition of cross-cultural weavings and needlework with an attendant book/catalog of the same title: ***The Birth Symbol in Traditional Women's Art from Europe and the Western Pacific*** (Toronto: The Museum for Textiles, 1981). He discusses "primitive art" and women's work. He quotes (on p. 8) **Douglas Fraser**, "Primitive art as it is understood today is not intended to serve aesthetic ends... either [these works] assist in ritual or they perform a social role... Thus the Western idea of art for art's sake would mean little to the primitive artist." He then quotes **Joseph Fischer**'s *Threads of Tradition— Textiles of Indonesia and Sarawak*: "Labor-saving devices for producing traditional cloths would be by definition meaningless.... In traditional terms there are no shortcuts to producing a fine textile." Finally, quoting **William Irwin Thompson**'s *The Time Falling Bodies Take to Light* (1981) about the time of Goddess worship: "Women may look to a golden age of close, intimate, and peaceful village life, but men tremble in visions of asphyxiation and extinction in the herd. As C.S. Lewis has expressed the male nightmare: 'You may add that in the hive and the anthill we see fully realized the two things that some of us most dread for our own species—the dominance of the female and the dominance of the collective.' Man cut the umbilical cord to the Great Mother with a sword, and the sword has been hanging over his head ever since."

The two together, the earth and what women can make of it, are magic.

We want to lead our lives so that what we make of what we find on earth is magic. The way to find it is in the ritual of patiently doing, over and over, what is required of the work. Frequently a knitter is asked, *"How long does it take to do that?"* though that question never arises in regard to jogging, movie-going, or mall shopping. If we choose not to join the patriarchy, what are our other choices? There is no set of procedures to follow to a become a conscious rebelling radical feminist. But a hunger exists which some try to feed by means of new-age spirituality, sensing that what is missing is what is holy. Some study Native Americans and try to imitate a past not their own, recognizing the integrity of that culture, an integrity which still exists amongst traditional people in pockets around the world. The question is how to find traditional women's work, healing, magic, and spirit when one is not a traditional woman.

We might suggest that the very simple work of sustaining life can have magic in it when we absent ourselves from the noise and rush of progress and technology. It is work and often tedious work to prepare food each day, to tend a garden and struggle with weeds and tomato hornworms, to care for each other, children and ourselves ... to make things, as in knitting, spinning, or weaving. When people ask about the time needed to produce a handmade object, it means they do not see that it is the act of making it which provides the "grounding," the stitch after stitch that are individual moments of possibility. That the finished product is useful and/or beautiful is an added satisfaction.[23] The training, work, and consciousness a potter, bas-

Pat Shea knitting.

In Selma's garden at home.

ketmaker or weaver possesses, skills with herbs and flowers or a frying pan are inherently satisfying and potentially of spiritual sustenance to the worker.

These activities are not, in our opinion, art. Patriarchal art is not supposed to be utilitarian. An artist expects that art lives in galleries and museums. An artist cannot help but partake of a world of elitism and a defense of pornography. The hierarchical structure of art and women's gratitude for crumbs of recognition leads many women artists into a defense of violence and cruelty, and a few to attempt to imitate it. Of course there are artists who produce work that is very moving to us, just as there are doctors who can sometimes help despite their training in dissociation and in treating the body as a battleground. It is a matter of joining the ranks of "educated men," as Virginia Woolf wrote in *Three Guineas*, whose values are individual and competitive, money-oriented and worshipful of violence. Art that "sells" will be rife with those values. And "artists," women among them, defend it all as "art."

Consider: Art and Sex as the icons of the 20th century—not to be criticized (beyond criticism).[24]

We try to stay outside the corridors of patriarchal power as much as possible. In fact, we believe the best way to have some measure of independence within the patriarchy is by creating a small business and we would encourage other women to do likewise. It is a means of making, at least to a degree, our own reality, and of attracting and encouraging others with similar values. But whether we choose professionalism or less admired work, we believe women hunger for and miss work that has meaning and integrity. If we can imagine women living in an older time or indigenous women living in areas all over the world now where "technology" is simple, then we can imagine work that maintained a woman's life and that of the community as being at least sometimes sacred, no matter how difficult.

24. Some would add the media. In the December 1992 issue of *Off our backs*, **nikki craft** wrote an article called "So Much Slime So Little Time" in which she says, "The media is the new church; the television its altar; the images its sacrament; the First Amendment its bible; and any critique its blasphemy."

We are constantly told that solutions to emptiness will be found in "progress," meaning more complex technologies; and then we don't realize that what we miss is the human element and what is real in the natural world. The work that is ordinary can be magical: saved seed sprouting and growing into food; sheep's wool or flax stalk being spun into a thread and that thread forming warp into which weft can be interlaced; clay-earth shaped into a container; strips of weeds or bark bent into a shape to carry. These "hard," tedious, repeated labors aren't necessarily sacred *per se*, but can bring us into a consonance with our lives on earth in an appropriate way. To quote again from Paula Gunn Allen:

25. Gunn Allen, op. cit., p. 24.

This brings me to the matter of the relation of ritual magic to women's lives and especially to the women's tradition: magic, as the word itself implies (ma-ge[c]), is primarily a womanly enterprise. Its closest kin are the domestic arts, and its chosen implements and procedures most closely resemble those developed by women to facilitate their tasks. It should surprise no one that the modern age, from its beginnings in the Renaissance to the present, has become more and more intensely patriarchal over the world and thus more and more thoroughly separated from womanity, from ritual magic, from tribal social systems, and from harmony with the earth. The four have ever danced together: woman, magic, tribes, and earth, and the dance goes on, even yet.[25]

26. Pete Hamill wrote an article in the November-December issue of *New Age Magazine* called "Crack and the Box" in which he hypothesizes that television is a mind-altering drug that prepares humans to require the kind of passivity available only from hard drugs. **Marie Winn**, author of *The Plug-in Drug: Television, Children, and the Family*, & *Children Without Childhood* (Viking-Penguin) makes a similar

TIME AND TECHNOLOGY. Time. Our time on earth is limited. If we spend time at work which robs us of all it can and gives nothing back, how many hours each week are lost? If we relax by numbing our minds with a machine like television or with computer games, then both work and "relaxation" time are lost to us forever. We think we have all the time in the world and are entitled to all the earth's resources. It is sad that we indiscriminately waste both. Much has been written about technology and its destructiveness to the environment, much less on its effects on our souls. The truth is our lives are limited, as are the earth's riches. We can't afford to waste either. Time spent in front of a TV,[26] time spent reading junk mail, time spent in shopping malls—all of it shortens our opportunities for real knowledge, real pleasure, and true spirituality.

We must exorcise the evils of patriarchy by recognizing them and naming them as Mary Daly has written. We need to realize that women, animals and the earth are being tortured and destroyed. But we also need ecstasy, a reconnection with that which restores our spirits. For us this often comes from the books we read, from the watching and tending life, both plant and animal. It comes from the gratification of preparing food well, spinning fibers or stories, knitting sweaters and relationships, weaving a matrix toward a future. How can women "reconstitute the world"?[27] It's a question we think about often, and encourage you to consider seriously also.

CELEBRATION. Vegetarianism is coming into style. More and more studies are showing its good effects on our health, and that is, of course, very good for our business. We are disappointed though when people only turn to vegetables out of fear of cholesterol instead of from a desire to celebrate. What's to celebrate? No killing, no cruelty, and the amazing diversity of grains and greens. Some think they will deprive themselves if they can't have it all, if they can't eat everything. However the deprivation doesn't lie there, the deprivation results from not having the opportunity to explore the alternatives.

Think of how few meats there are, and how few the ways they can be cooked: broiled, roasted, boiled, or fried. Think of what passes for vegetables on the plate beside the meat, then imagine just the grains—all the kinds of rice: white, basmati, Arborio, short-grain brown, and wild rice,[28] as well as millet, quinoa, barley, buckwheat groats, and of course, wheat. Think of the enormous cabbage family: of broccoli, Brussels sprouts and kale, Chinese cabbage, bok-choi, mustard greens, and collards. Think about the sweet roots: parsnips and carrots, turnips and beets. Think of the pulses: the peas and lentils and

argument. Others have reported negative effects from television: not just from its programming, but from its technology—most notably **Jerry Mander**: in the *Absence of the Sacred* (San Francisco: Sierra Club Books, 1992). He believe that TV (and satellite TV) is creating a world of zombies, a kind of drugged learning that functions the way speed does on the nervous system. It is obvious to many that TV destroys human attention span. Both television and computers are "antithetical to information sources that traditional societies have used" (Mander, p. 59). Mander also points our that automation and computerization have destroyed entry level as well as other jobs. This excellent book is an exposé of "progress" as well as a call to stop the destruction of indigenous peoples' cultures.

27. "I have to cast my lot with those who age after age, perversely, with no extraordinary power, reconstitute the world." From *The Dream of a Common Language* by **Adrienne Rich**. (New York: W.W. Norton, 1978).

28. Wild rice, *Zizania aquatica* is not a true rice, but a tall aquatic grass distantly related to

cultivated rice. It is a staple Of the Chippewa people, in the Great Lakes region.

29. An awe of what we have to celebrate and why, is beautifully communicated by **Elizabeth Dodson Gray** in an article entailed "Seeing & Hearing the Living Earth" in *Woman of Power*, issue 20, Spring 1991.

beans in amazing numbers. Think of the chickpea flour dumplings of India and all the gravies called dahls. Until we forgo the meats and the television, we don't have time or space to discover, to learn, to celebrate. When we forgo the shopping mall and throw out the TV, we have time to learn the earth's riches, its spirit, its plants and creatures and people, and time to read the books that can engage our mind the way the flickering dots on the computer screens never can.

Everything alive changes. It either grows or fades. Perennials spread; sometimes they die out in the center and need to be divided. Sometimes they die and their seeds continue their race. And some plants and creatures become extinct. Those of us who treasure diversity try to keep as many kinds of life going as possible, and that is how we try to live our lives: encouraging growth and life, a spirit and way of living that is perennial life. Celebrate life![29] ✺

*Bloodroot on vacation:
Cel Noll, Selma, Liz Seaborn.*

Noel.

Personal Essays

1993–2013

In addition to the essays written for their cookbooks, Selma and Noel wrote essays for publication in feminist journals and magazines. Since 2011, Selma periodically posts to her blog Selma's List, *selmaslist.blogspot.com*, also accessible through the Bloodroot website, *bloodroot.com*.

From a pamphlet in Bloodroot's archives:

"When one stops playing the slave's game, the world falls apart. Nothing is left. Nothing that one learned before works anymore. How does one walk, talk, dress, play, think, love, differently? Each minute, how and what does one do? The world becomes a very dangerous place. When one stops playing the slave's game, one must start to invent every minute of one's life. There are no forms which already exist to show how, and there are no liberated communities where exemplary people lead exemplary lives. One lives on the edge of a personal world collapsed, in direct opposition to the whole world of reality and power, and what then can one do except invent?"

—*Andrea Dworkin*

"*Marx and Gandhi were Liberals—Feminism & the 'Radical' Left.*" Adapted from an article originally published in *American Report*, 1973. Republished by Frog In The Well, Palo Alto, CA: "*Frog in the Well is a collective publishing & distributing short, inexpensive pamphlets covering a broad range of topics.*"

Her mother Therese, & Noel.

Her Life & Mine

Originally published in *Lesbian Ethics* Volume 5 No. 1: *Lesbians & Our Mothers*, 1993.

I AM 48 NOW, two years older than my mother was when she died. It's strange not having her out there in front of me any more. Throughout my life I had thought, *this is what she was doing at my age and how different I am.* Or, *how much the same we are.* Now she is not there for me as that given against which to measure myself. It used to be that mostly I thought I was doing it better than she had, measure for measure. That was before she died. I still think it is true, but *how* I think it has changed.

So then to go back.

My mother Therese was nineteen when I was born. She was the seventh of seven sisters of an Irish-French mother and a German father. The story goes that her family was quite well-to-do. All the daughters went to private Catholic boarding schools until the stock market crash when her father lost a fortune. My mother was a little girl then. It must have been hard for *her* mother to cope with the combination of financial disaster, a husband in a T.B. sanatorium and the work of caring for her youngest daughter, Therese. Because her six sisters before her had gone to Catholic boarding schools with the Order of the Sacred Heart, the nuns decided that my mother could attend their prestigious school free of charge. She was in their care from the age of four until she graduated from high school. I understand that there were some summers and holidays when she stayed at school since going home was impossible for reasons that are still unclear to me. According to family and school reports, Therese was considered brilliant and difficult. I was 26 when she died. How she died is hard to talk about. It was many years before I came to understand the pain—both hers and mine.

My mother Therese married my father when she was 18 years old, having just graduated from high school. He was 19 and in the airforce. It was 1943. I was born in 1944. I don't have any clear early memories of her, but there are pictures, and she was a beautiful young woman. From those pictures I can also see that she loved me, her first baby. I don't know when things started going bad for her. After my birth? Or that of my first brother? The earliest memory of trouble that I have dates to when I was 3 or 4 years old. We were in Oregon in a logging camp. There was a period when she kept the curtains closed on all the windows of our cabin. And then one day her pajamas caught on fire. From the pot-bellied stove? The cause was never entirely clear but I knew that she had set the fire. I'm not sure how I knew. I think it was something my father said as he struggled to put out the flames.

Sometime after that she flew East to New York City. My brother, my father and I took a train across the country shortly thereafter to be with her on the East Coast so that she could see the psychiatrist here who was to eventually make her "well."

I have no memories of emotional difficulties for my mother for several years following our arrival on the East Coast except for those long periods of time when the curtains closed out the daylight. Then a third child was born and shortly thereafter, a fourth. My mother told me at a later date that her psychiatrist had warned my father that she would be unable to cope with more children. And it was after this younger brother and sister were born that what had come to be known as my mother's "mental illness" began to coalesce. Certainly it became a vivid reality for me.

Now, I can remember adoring my mother with all the passion possible in the heart of a two year old girl. I wanted her to love me. I wanted to be absorbed completely by the wonder of her. The later years of pain and anger all but smothered that original and deeper passion.

Noel.

The pain began to be conscious for me when I was thirteen or so. Three things happened that year. I am not sure of the sequence but each had enormous impact.

My mother was extremely beautiful according to whatever were the standards then. There is a story that a Hollywood talent agent "discovered" her when she was a child and wanted to make her a star. Her family forbade it—apparently it was beneath the dignity of her upperclass background. So in my thirteenth year, she decided that I and my brother would become models. And I would become and fulfill her dreams.

I had mixed feelings regarding my work as a model. On the one hand, I was flattered that I should be thought of as "pretty enough." At 13, I found it was exciting to take the train to New York City for bookings and professional children's school. On the other hand, I was very self-conscious, and often subject to harassment from

Noel modeling in a Kotex ad.

the photographers. It had been my mother who had made me vulnerable to this painful reality. I felt betrayed by her though at the time I had no words for it. The thought itself was barely formed. I was only conscious of a deep discomfort. I know now she was teaching me to become a woman in the way she thought she had wanted for herself. Though she did not understand it, that way was part of what destroyed her.

Also, that year, my younger brother almost died. The doctor didn't believe the danger he was in but my mother knew and her fear was palpable. Still, she took command, ordered my father to fill the tub with cold water and ice and then held my brother in the freezing water till his 107° fever came down. This moment of strength is vivid in my mind but I think the strain of it cost her dearly.

The third event I remember was my mother's "nervous breakdown." My father took her to Fairfield Hills State Mental Hospital. She was weak and begging not to be taken away. I don't know what she did to warrant being committed to an institution. It was one of many times that such an event would shake my world and hers.

Why did these events happen? And what was her pain about? As I think about it now, I see her situation as not so very different from that of many women. In her case, she had not learned how to survive even minimally. She was terrified of much that I take for granted. She couldn't drive a car; she was afraid to go grocery shopping alone. The fact that she was beautiful weakened her further because she believed that her beauty would bring her happiness and that men would love her and take care of her because of it. But her beauty did not make her whole. And, because of her upperclass background, she expected others to do for her what most of us take for granted we will do for ourselves. Whatever capacity she had for growth was diminished by both her class expectations and by her beauty. She was "manic-depressive" and, though I didn't know it at the time, an alcoholic. She took tranquilizers and she tried to kill herself with terrifying regularity.

Through my teen years, my anger and contempt grew deeper as my mother grew more and more self-destructive. I was in a rage that she was destroying herself. I hated her for what she was doing to me and for what she was trying to do to herself.

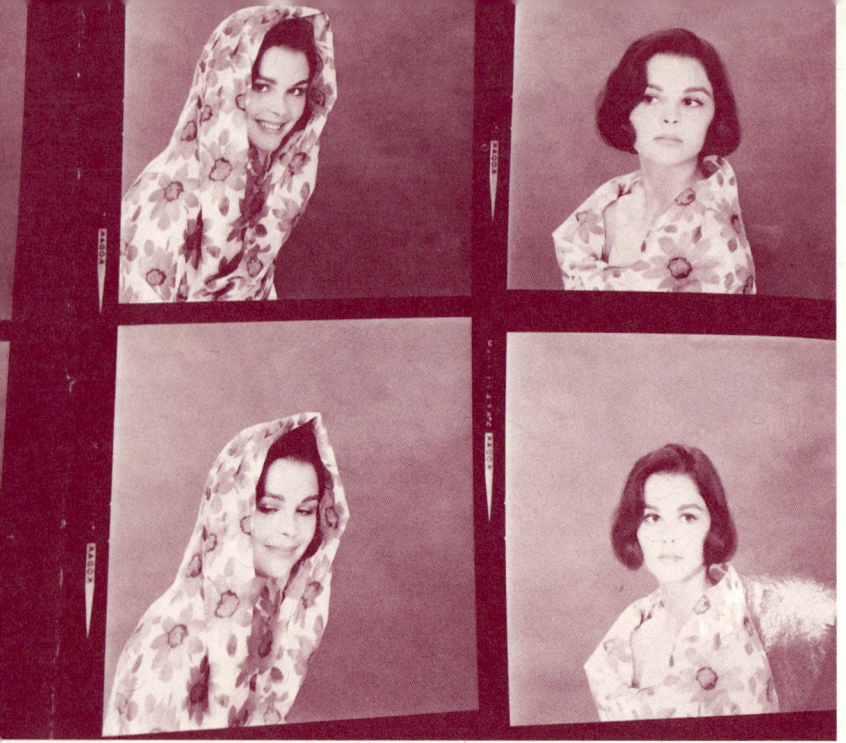

The door to what had been a passionate love for her was shut so tight that I couldn't feel any of her pain.

My mother stayed married to my father for 17 years. She told me that she had hated him much of that time and I remember that he was a coward and cruel to her when she was most vulnerable. At the time I was sure that I wouldn't ever do anything so wasteful of my life as to stay in an unhappy marriage. When I got married myself, I knew it wasn't forever. But it was unhappy and it was for ten years. And it was remembering how bad her life had been that made me change mine. By then, she had died.

My mother divorced my father when I was 16. She thought that my brother and I could support her and our younger siblings with our modeling. Her drinking and her use of tranquilizers continued and it became clear that she couldn't take care of four children. For my part, I resented her wanting me to work to take care of her. Eventually, there were court orders, child custody battles and interviews with child welfare people: my father ended up with custody of the four of us and my mother was devastated.

It was after having had children of my own and facing the possibility of losing them because I am a Lesbian that I came

Noel modeling, 1961.

to realize what the reality of losing her children had meant to her. At the time I tried to tell her it was alright, we'd visit her, call and so on. Now my own experience as a mother informs my understanding of the depth of her pain and humiliation.

In the years that followed, I graduated from high school and went to work in New York City. Various people took care of my mother during those years. Sometimes her family stepped in, sometimes a boyfriend or a friend. Sometimes I'd get a call from one of these people that Therese was in Fairfield Hills or sometimes the call would be from her: "Noelly, come help me." Then I would go to find her, with blood all over the house or threatening to overdose on her tranquilizers. I got sick of it.

Shortly after I was married, my mother re-married. Her new husband was a doctor with a decidedly sadistic streak. According to one of her sisters, he injected her with speed in their bedroom. She, for her part, tried to burn his house down. (I loved it that she had done that. I saw it as a rare act of rebellion on her part.)

I was 26 when my mother died. I had had my first child, a girl. My mother had married a third time and was living in Washington, DC with her new husband. How she died is difficult to talk about, but I will.

My mother's husband had gone to "dry out" at an alcoholic retreat. She had refused to go with him. She stayed in their apartment, and got drunk. Then she tore around the place in what must have been an incredible rage destroying everything that he treasured. After a time, she passed out and suffocated in her own vomit. And so, finally, she destroyed herself.

A YEAR AFTER my mother died, I had another child. I found myself depressed as she had been. Unhappy in marriage as she had been. And I thought, I don't want my life to go on like this—so much like hers. This was in the early '70s, feminism had started its "second wave." And I became a part of that second wave. It was at this time that I was able to begin to heal the pain between my mother and me.

Long before she died, I had left my mother. I closed the gate to the source of my passion for her because if it were left open, I could not survive her self-destruction. I had to close her out and in so doing I closed myself in. After she died, I began to know that a part of me had been lost to myself and that this loss was as painful as the loss of her. I felt deeply that I must learn to love her again. She was the source of my life. In whatever ways she failed me, I needed to understand that the responsibility was not hers but had the oppressive condition of women as its source.

It was five years after my mother died that I became a lesbian. I'm not sure that I would have had the strength to go against her will in such a manner if she had lived. Her energy and influence over me were very, very powerful. But she did die and in dying freed me to see her life and my need for my own.

I adored my first lesbian lover in the way that I adored my mother when I was two years old. I wanted this woman to take care of me as my mother hadn't. She couldn't of course, nor did she want to take care of me in the way I thought I needed. Now I am grateful, though at the time all I could feel was rejection. Because I loved her and didn't want to lose her, I needed to find a way for us to have an adult and mutually respectful relationship. It was a long hard struggle during which I learned I had to take care of myself and to love myself. I feel very, very fortunate that she and I got through that stage of our knowing each other. We survived those changes and are now long-time intimates and cronies together.

I came to clear my guilt in regard to my mother with the help of my first lover and other lesbians with whom I was close. I remember one evening when four of us were looking through my family albums. The pictures there reveal the anger, tensions, and the jealousies—as pictures will. It came as a great surprise that I had never really seen what was so obvious that night. Up until that moment I had always felt guilty about my anger toward my mother. Everyone else seemed to think her wonderful. She herself often said that I didn't love her enough; that she had loved *her* mother much, much more. That night I saw my mother and me through the eyes of my lesbian friends and I knew that my anger toward her had been justified. I remember some of those times with her in which I had felt humiliated or in which I had shut down from the emotions caused by her self-destructiveness.

Through the years that followed my feminist perspective deepened and my anger toward my mother began to change. During that time I realized that I needed to see our situation

(hers and mine) differently—in a political context—so that
I could grow beyond the anger into something constructive.
I had a sense that if I couldn't do that, i.e., couldn't create
something constructive in myself in regard to my relationship
with my mother, then some part of what is spiritual about me,
my longing for the Earth and some connection to it, would be
lost. Her body, her female body, was and is both a metaphor
and real, symbol and actuality, for the Earth and life. How
destroyed her spirit was and therefore how destructive she was
towards me is a concrete example of the result of patriarchy's
constant attacks on all that is female and sacred. I felt I had to
take her back again to heal the wounds we had inflicted upon
each other. This healing goes on still, as our relationship does.
I learned that my mother was a woman who had been taught,
as all women have been taught, to pass her pain on down to her
daughter. The patriarchy insists on it. I thought of the specifics
of her life: how much of a victim she had been and how much
self-hate she had learned. My anger abated.

Over the next several years I found myself talking frequently
with my lover about my mother. In her presence I was able to
gradually open my heart to my grief. There were nights when
the memory of my mother came flooding in and I would find
myself sobbing, grieving at last, for my own loss and also for all
the pain in her life.

So it was as a lesbian and with the support of other lesbians
that I began to love my mother again. It was through my close
and long-term intimate relationships with lesbians that I
learned to trust. Lesbian women had confirmed my anger and
understood on the deepest level the degree of pain which had
existed between my mother and me. With my anger freed, I was
able to understand the cause of my pain and then finally, after
several more years, to truly mourn the loss of my mother—to
herself, to me, to this earth.

I have a wooden doll made by a woman from Quebec. She
arrived through the mail several years back. She looks like my
mother did when I was young. So she is my mother and I have
made my peace with her, through her. I told her that she had
to behave herself. No self-destruction. No drinking. None of
that funny business with the razor blades. And she has agreed
because she wants to live. And she does. In me. ✪

*Adrienne Rich at Bloodroot.
From left: Noel, Pat Shea, Adrienne Rich,
Selma, Betsey Beaven.*

Selma.

Selma Miriam

A Consideration of the Domestic Arts: Fiberwork, Cooking, Gardening

Reflections on a Feminist Weaver's Life.
A talk given at a meeting of the Connecticut Weaver's Guild, 2013.

I WENT TO HIGH SCHOOL in Bridgeport, CT, and while there, I had a very demanding but charismatic biology teacher. As a result, I decided that I wanted to learn what was the secret of life and would therefore major in biology in college. The school I went to was Tufts, and I didn't realize how much of a premed school it was. The girls' part, Jackson, admitted only a third the number compared to the liberal arts, and so girls who majored in biology often got better grades than the boys, who felt that the girls were there for their MRS degrees while the boys were there to become doctors. This was the 1950s.

I also had a father who had a fabric store and who loved quality textiles. He often brought home remnants of brocades or silks, or fine wools—not exactly the sort of stuff to clothe a teenager. (My mother had made my clothes until I was old enough to sew my own. Of course I absorbed my father's admiration, and I went off to college with my Bernina sewing machine. But I did not yet know how to type!)

Once I got to college, I decided that more of the secret of life lay in the study of psychology than in biology, and I ended up with something of a double major, and honors in both biology and psychology.

I did love college. But I have to tell you that the best thing that I learned there was how to knit. Since I was on the dean's list, I could audit any class I wanted for no extra charge. Since neither of my parents had graduated from high school, this great opportunity of cramming as much as possible into my education was desirable. But—I needed to be able to take reflective notes from so much material, and knitting helped. I would ask each professor if it was okay to knit. The science ones said *Sure, as long as you can keep up with the work.* (Remember, they wanted to weed out the girls from the boys.) The Humanities professors sometimes said no. Knitting taught me how to listen before I slavishly wrote everything down. Best of all, since Tufts had so many international students, I could learn "continental" knitting, where one picks the yarn instead of throwing it. In those days we were making argyle socks, with k2p2 cuffs, and it was very good to not have to drag the yarn back and forth to do this, and to be able to use both hands equally.

Knitting is still a central part of my life. I'm a very impatient person, and any required wait time makes me crazy. My solace, my patience always comes from knitting a row or two.

I had planned to go to graduate school, but was interrupted by an unexpected pregnancy (due to a doctor's failed contraceptive device), and with baby and husband moved to a miserable part of the southeast Bronx. All of a sudden I had no class schedule to follow for the first time in my 22 years, and no homework. I was at a loss. I needed some science projects. So I trekked to the local library with a baby in a stroller once a week, to take out cookbooks (to the dismay of my husband, who thought he was marrying an intellectual). Each week I would laboriously copy out recipes by hand that I wanted to try—my science projects. And on occasion, they were good enough to eat.

I went on sewing, of course, and I tried to get morning glory seeds to sprout and grow on my window sill. (I envied tenants who had fire escapes in the sun, not me.)

I was quite miserable despite my efforts at homemaking, and after 4 years, my parents intervened. Because I needed a garden by this time, and with my parents' help, we bought a little Cape Cod type house in Westport CT for $15,000 and I made my first garden in 1962.

Once there, I was so intent on gardening that I decided to learn how to design them, and did so for other people for about 20 years. I was less interested in choosing plant material for

The squash patch at Bloodroot.

other people, but I liked determining outdoor spaces, how to make outdoor rooms, how to get privacy, walks through a woods, surprise spaces, and adequate parking. I joined the American Rock Garden Society. The members there were less interested in English style formal borders and succession of bloom. Instead they wanted to try to please rare plants from all over the world. As a result, their gardens were unique, quirky, and unusual. I loved going to see them.

At the same time I was still cooking, and wanting to learn about foods from other peoples from all over the world. Comfort foods.

Sometime in the 1970s, along came feminism. I had always been angry with sexism as applied to me and other women. Now there was a context, and many other women and a few men, who were discussing, writing, marching, and protesting.

But what to do besides be angry? Some women in the '70s went back to school to become professionals. I could have done so too— my husband, a lawyer, wanted me to do that. But I was suspicious that my values and spirit would be co-opted by joining a profession—and remember, what I loved—the gardening, cooking, knitting—none of those fit a professional description. I loved designing gardens, but I didn't particularly like most of my clientele.

Virginia Woolf wrote compellingly about all this in her book *Three Guineas*. For those of you who haven't read it, or who read it too long ago to remember: in the late 1930s, she was asked to contribute money (guineas) to three different charities—an anti-war group, a women's college, and a women's professional organization. The book has been considered an anti-war tract, which it certainly was—but it is more importantly a feminist work. She considers herself, and all women, as outsiders to the patriarchy. She writes about the situation of the daughters of educated men vs. the sons of educated men. And at one point she says:

As you know from your own experience... the daughters... have always done their thinking from hand to mouth; not under green lamps at study tables in the cloisters of secluded colleges. They have thought while they stirred the pot, while they rocked the cradle . . . Let us never cease from thinking—what is this 'civilization' in which we find ourselves? What are these ceremonies and why should we take part in them? What are these professions and why should we make money out of them? Where in short is it leading us, the procession of the sons of educated men?

Later she says: *In fact, as a woman, I have no country. As a woman, I want no country. As a woman, my country is the whole world.*

I decided that I wanted to open a women's center. In the '70s, there were almost 200 women's bookstores around the country, and I wanted to open one as well, but I wanted to serve food, employing my fondness for different people's cuisines. There was a Feminist Bookstore Network (FBN), and a feminist music distributor called Women in Distribution (WIND).

Now I need to digress to tell you that there are precious few of these bookstores left. There was a famous one in Minneapolis, called Amazon, and Steve Bezos stole their name (giving them a pittance when they sued) and as I'm sure you all know, developed a business plan that made independent bookstores and the small publishers who depended on them almost extinct.

We still sell books, a few, and subsidize the bookstore with our restaurant. We decided that our feminism would inform all our business decisions. We would be different from upscale restaurants and even from health food restaurants in that we were and are animal rights vegetarians. Some of our differences: we have no chef—though we have cooks—not trained in culinary schools. We have no waitstaff. We share recipes—no secrets! Our decisions are made collectively. Of course we use local produce in season, and a lot of our cookbooks are written with seasonal chapters. We use organic vegetables as often as possible, and we won't carry anything produced by the exploitation of humans or other animals. We appreciate and treasure the cuisines of other people, and the wisdom. For example: of using a clay pot (an *olla de barro*—a Mexican idea) to cook beans, or a bamboo steamer for sticky rice, as Asian women do. We not only appreciate these techniques and foods, but we promote them, so that others can respect them and share them. We are less interested in the health food fads of the day. In the last 37 years they have changed many times—such as a devotion to yoghurt, honey, and whole wheat in 1977, to raw and gluten free now. Of course we had whole wheat (our own bread), yoghurt, and honey then, and we have gluten free and raw (salads) now—it's just not part of our larger purpose!

Now sometimes folks ask, how are your precepts different from humanism, or environmentalism, or animal rights, and we say, we may have much or all in common, but we came to these decisions from our understanding of feminism.

Selma's Mermaid Quilt.

And how does this all apply to weaving? I'm about to get there. In the mid '80s, a quilter came into the restaurant. She got me excited about the idea of using scraps of fabric to make tessellations. It seemed like such a frugal, womanly thing to do! I decided that if Escher could design tessellations with male figures, I could do female ones. It was much harder than I expected, and took over a year, but I designed a mermaid quilt, machine pieced, hand quilted. And it took 9 years to complete, and now hangs on a rafter at Bloodroot.

Then there was an article in *Threads* magazine on knitting lace. I wrote and asked, *where would one buy fine yarn?* (I didn't know a weaver.) They answered, *Well, you could spin it!* Next, a customer came in with a spare copy of *Spin Off*. It had an ad for a Schacht Matchless Wheel—a small castle wheel—and since I wasn't interested in historical reenactments and wasn't charmed by the design of the Saxony wheel, but this little tidy wheel looked just right for my Cape Cod house. So I ordered one, though I didn't know how to spin! Impulsive! But it did seem to be magic, to be able to make thread. And now I have four spinning wheels in my small living room.

In the late '80s—maybe 1989 or 1990, SOAR (Spin Off Autumn Retreat) was held in upstate New York. We had been used to closing for vacation in the fall, and we decided to see how this retreat was. I wondered how a group of feminist lesbians would be received by spinners. Well, it was wonderful. We were very warmly welcomed. Dale Pettigrew had been asked by Linda Ligon (Interweave Press owner) to shape SOAR, and everything about it reflected Dale's feminism and earth centered spirituality. It suited us, (except the resort food) and we continued to go, every year, for 12 years.[1] At SOAR I not only learned to spin all the varieties of animal fiber but also linen and cotton. And of course natural dye classes. I asked Rita Buchanan what to do with linen and cotton and she said, *I guess you'll have to learn to weave.* And so, I asked Mary Gunn to teach me. A little later, Noel learned also.

And what would feminist weaving be like? For me, it has been at least respecting and/or trying to do the kind of weaving

1. We stopped going to SOAR after 2002. We were worried about closing the restaurant in the fall, when we were still somewhat busy, and decided instead to close for vacation in February, the slowest month for us.

Selma's garden at home.

from around the world—whether backstrap from Southern Peru, or hand weaving of the Scandinavian countries. Sometimes it is subject matter, when I decided to weave mermaids on my dobby loom.

I prefer to use natural dyes rather than aniline dyes. *What comes from the Earth shall not harm the Earth.* When I am doing what is, in my opinion, my best work, it is like this: it is my own design. It is woven from my own handspun, and dyed with natural colors. Not all my work is like this, but sometimes I do at least some pieces this way. Right now I am working on napkins from a name draft [fellow guild member] Julia Ludlow-Ortner developed by means of her computer and I like it fine, even though, for me, there is a loss of agency by using these solutions to design.

It seems to me that when I have seen a body of a weaver's work, it is an expression of who she, or he, is. I sometimes go to Jackie Heller's house, and all of it—her stencils on the walls, the table runners, baskets she has made, and her garden are intensely about her and her husband—similarly to Deborah Dudly's felted owl. I expect that if I visited any of you I would have a similar reaction to seeing your very unique and particular magic.

In my search for the secret or the meaning of life, I found some answers or let's say explanation of what pleases me in Paula Gunn Allen's book *Grandmothers of the Light*. Part Lebanese and part Laguna Sioux, what she writes explains to me why knitting, weaving, weeding a garden, making baskets or pottery are so gratifying to those of us who do them. She studies the word *mage*—one who does magic, and this is what she says:

The basic nature of the universe of power is magic: the name given to the practice of a mage. Ma . . . comes in variants: ma, mo, mu, mi, and me. All are version of the same morpheme...and refer one way or another to the Great Mother or Great Goddess . . . named variously Ma, or Maat . . . and known even today . . . as Tiamat, Aphrodite, Ishtar, Astarte, and Isis. She can be discerned in words such as mother, mom, mammary, mutter . . . Ma is the essential female syllable . . . and at its root designates mystery, mother, and much, all feminine forces or powers. Ge, another fragment, one from which words such as geology . . . geometry, geophysics, and geopolitical derive, is the name of Gaia. . . and refers to those of the Great Goddesses' powers that emanate from her planetary body. . . (that is, the Earth!)

A mage is a shaman or medicine person... Magic refers to the ritual activities of a mage... ritual actions that result in transformations.

 Examples of these transformations—fiber into thread, thread into weaving. Seed becoming grain, grain into flour, and then bread. These transformations of what the earth gives us are magic.
 So at last I had found the secret of life, or at least, what makes life wonderful for me. I assume that all of you have also experienced the excitement, the rush of suddenly knowing just what you want to make—having learned a new technique or weave structure, and while there may be mistakes or disappointments as the project progresses, there is the thrill of the interaction with the threads, the pleasure in working with one's own hands, the surprise of lifting a skein out of an indigo bath and watching it turn blue in front of you as you look.
 And for me, there's the burst of a seed becoming a seedling, growing my own indigo, or the feel of the bread dough—and these days, making cultured cheese from cashews. Such a glorious, satisfying way to live, making magic! ✹

Anniversary party at Bloodroot, 1980s, from left: Sandy Anderson, Selma, Donna Osborne, Alicia Woodson, Meg Profetto, Betsey Beaven, Noel.

First offset edition reprint © 2020
1,000 copies
ISBN 978-1-7346315-0-0
Alder & Frankia

The original Alder & Frankia book was edited, designed, risograph printed, & handbound by Emily Larned at her studio RCHQ in Bridgeport, CT.

First printing: 2017. 200 signed & numbered copies 1–200, risograph printed & handbound by Emily, no ISBN.

Second printing: 2018. 200 signed & numbered copies 201–400, risograph printed by Emily, handbound by Emily & studio assistant Qianying Niu, no ISBN.

© 2017, 2020, this collection. Copyright of individual works revert to the original authors, who encourage reproduction, properly credited, "for feminist and vegetarian purposes."

THANK YOU
To Selma & Noel for generously providing the material for this book. To Manuscripts & Archives, Yale University Library, for making their Bloodroot Collective Records (MS 1955) publicly accessible. To the many enthusiastic & patient pre-orders who supported the production costs of the first printing. To SJ for editing help with an earlier, abandoned version of this book. To my fellow artist bookmakers—Bridget, Aaron, Tate; and my Bpt Crit Group—Caroline, Crystal, Richard; who helped troubleshoot and encourage this book into being. To my mom for driving me to Bloodroot when I was 16, and to Sarah for the initial recommendation. To the University of Connecticut for contributing support to this edition. And to Chris for everything else.

ALDER & FRANKIA (est. 2016): Alder & Frankia publications are collaborations and reissues of feminist material.

The alder is a birch tree that flourishes in unexpected places thanks to its symbiotic relationship with the microorganism frankia, which lives in its roots. The alder feeds the frankia sugar, and in return the frankia converts nitrogen into a compound that enables the alder to thrive.

Alder & Frankia is a project by artist-publisher Emily Larned, who is co-founder of Impractical Labor in Service of the Speculative Arts (ILSSA). She is Assistant Professor of Graphic Design at the University of Connecticut, Storrs.

A note on the type: This book is set in the diverse family of **Eskorte**, the debut typeface of designer Elena Schneider. A very readable and serviceable textface in its regular version, the lively italics of its heavier weights recall 1970s typography. Studious yet spirited, reminiscent of the '70s yet also thoroughly contemporary, designed by a woman: Eskorte seems to me the perfect typeface for a book on Bloodroot.

A note on the paper: This book is printed on Dur-O-Tone, by the French Paper Company. French Paper is a sixth-generation family-owned and operated paper company in Niles, Michigan. The French Paper Company employs onsite hydropower to produce all of their paper.

A note on the printing: printed offset with 100% windpower in Maine.

Alder & Frankia
RCHQ
1069 Connecticut Ave #4-310
Bridgeport, CT 06607
USA

emily.k.larned@gmail.com
emilylarned.com
impractical-labor.org